The Shattered Crown

Machelle Flory

DEDICATION

This, my first book, is dedicated to my grandmother. She encouraged me to write simply because I wanted to, and she never doubted that I could.

Thank you, Grandma. I love you.

Contents

PROLOGUE:

The storm had been gathering since dusk, coiling above the capital like a vast, patient beast. Lightning stitched the heavens in jagged white veins, crawling over the spires of the High Palace, yet the rain refused to fall. The wind carried a low, unnatural hum, deep and thrumming, vibrating through stone and bone alike, as though the very air had sensed what was about to unfold.

Queen Elara felt it.

The Crown of Echoes, resting light yet impossibly heavy upon her brow. Beneath its silver filigree, five inner lights flickered, one for each united kingdom, wavering, restless, as if whispering a warning she could not fully hear. She slowed in the corridor outside the throne hall and lifted a hand, her fingers brushing the crown's edge.

Something is wrong.

Something has already begun.

Footsteps sounded behind her, measured, confident, achingly familiar. A royal guard emerged from the shadows, clad in full ceremonial steel, his helmet casting his eyes into darkness. He bowed, precise and practiced, just as every loyal guard had bowed since the day she had taken the throne.

"Your Majesty," he said.

It was not the words, but the emptiness behind them, the smoothness, the lack of warmth, that sent a chill sliding down her spine.

She turned.

Too late – everything moved slowly.

Steel flashed. Pain bloomed, sharp, blinding, absolute. The assassin drove the blade into her ribs from behind, the force ripping the breath from her lungs. Elara gasped and staggered forward as warmth soaked her gown, her hand clawing blindly for support until her fingers struck stone.

The guard stepped around her. His face remained hidden. His silence was a verdict.

Thunder cracked overhead.

"You..." she rasped, struggling to breathe. "Who sent you?"

He did not answer.

Her knees struck the marble. Cold bit into her palms as the world began to tilt and blur. Pain crept higher into her chest, squeezing, stealing. She felt her life loosening its grip, felt the Crown of Echoes shudder against her brow, vibrating, frantic, aware that its bearer was dying.

The assassin knelt beside her.

With calm, practiced precision, he drove the blade into her throat.

"For the Wraith King," he whispered.

Elara fell.

The world smeared into color and sound, blood on her tongue, thunder in her ears, her heartbeat faltered. She heard the Crown's hum turning frantic, wild.

And in that final moment, understanding dawned.

If she died as she was, the Crown could remain whole. It would pass, clean and intact, to the next rightful heir of her blood.

And he would claim it.

Better chaos, she thought.

Better ruin.

Better a *broken* world *than one* devoured by his *evil.*

With the last trembling spark of strength left in her failing body, Queen Elara lifted her blood-slicked hand, seized the Crown of Echoes, and tore it from her head.

The assassin froze, realization dawning on him far too late.

"No, "

She brought the Crown down upon the marble floor.

The sound that followed was not metal shattering, but the world itself breaking.

Light erupted through the hall, white and gold, black and crimson, violet fire, five distinct shards screaming outward, tearing through stone, sky, and storm as they streaked toward the far reaches of the Five Kingdoms.

Far to the north, in the frost-bitten Royal Peaks, the High Priestess jolted awake as the mountain shuddered beneath her. Lanterns guttered and died. The air sharpened, brittle as glass. She felt the fracture, not of crown or stone, but of destiny itself.

Words long buried rose unbidden to her lips:

When crown breaks by sovereign's hand,

the void uncoils and seeks the land.

Back in the palace, as the light faded, the assassin stood motionless beside the queen's still form. Horror hollowed his breath.

This was not the plan.

"What have you done?" he whispered.

But Queen Elara did not answer.

Her eyes had already closed.

And at that very moment, the world began to change.

CHAPTER ONE
The Crown Shatters

The Memory Market always smelled of rain, even on the driest days, ozone and wet stone clinging to the air like a promise that something was about to break.

Formally, it was called the Market of Whispers. It had been born generations ago, when the Crown first granted the Royal Archivists dominion over the nation's memories. What began as a sanctioned tool of interrogation soon slipped its leash. Beyond palace walls, in forgotten courtyards and shuttered back rooms, rogue mages learned to distill memory into glass vials, capturing moments as swirling light and color. It was a perilous art, one that blurred the boundary between magic and theft, between consent and violation.

Those who practiced the craft began calling themselves weavers. They extracted memories from willing minds, and from those with no choice at all. Secrets became currency. Regret could be erased. Pain could be bottled and bartered. People sold pieces of themselves simply to survive.

Many who came were desperate. Others were greedy. Some, like Lira, had nowhere else to go.

The Royal Archivists had tried more than once to burn the Market out, but too many powerful hands were dipped into its profits. Nobles paid to erase indiscretions. Criminals sold memories to forget the blood on their hands. Lovers traded their pasts for silence. And the clever weavers, especially the clever ones, knew which memories could be resold for leverage, blackmail, or ruin.

So the Market endured.

It became the only place where a person could disappear entirely, or uncover a truth someone else would gladly kill to keep buried. Some memories were worth more than gold, and the weavers were always willing to pay.

Lira kept her hood low as she slipped between the rows of lantern-lit stalls, every heartbeat drumming the same warning over and over:

Don't look anyone in the eyes. You don't know what you've sold.

The Market hummed with whispers, some spoken, others stolen. Glass vials glimmered from every stall, each holding a fragment of a life: a first kiss, a childhood triumph, a murder someone wanted forgotten. Buyers bargained in murmurs. Sellers smiled too wide, too eager.

Lira kept walking.

Her pockets were almost empty again. She'd sworn she was finished selling memories after the last time, but hunger had a way of negotiating on your behalf.

She stopped at a booth veiled in silver curtains. The weaver inside didn't bother to look up.

"Back again?" His voice slid like oil. "What will it be this time? A holiday? A heartbreak?" A pause. "Your real name?"

"I told you," Lira muttered. "I'm done."

The ground trembled before he could reply.

A low hum rolled through the Market, rattling bottles and iron lanterns. Conversations died mid-breath. Light wavered, as if even the flames were afraid.

Then the sky cracked.

A pillar of white fire tore upward from the direction of the palace, tearing the clouds apart. Five shards of blazing light burst outward, streaking across the night like falling stars.

Screams erupted. Some clutched their children. Others reached skyward, faces split between awe and terror.

One shard veered.

Straight toward Lira.

She staggered back as the world slowed, the light twisting, searching, choosing. It struck her chest with the force of a hammer. Pain exploded through her skull, a thousand voices crying out at once.

She fell to her knees.

The voices vanished as suddenly as they'd come, leaving only a ringing void. Lira knelt in the dirt as the Market dissolved into chaos.

Stalls toppled. People fled clutching their heads, their children, their stolen lives. Glass shattered on the cobblestones, memories spilling out like ghosts. A man reeled as sensations not his own washed over him, a newborn's cry, a battlefield scream, a moonlit kiss. He gagged, fleeing from the phantom sensations, feelings that didn't belong to him.

None of it felt real.

Not compared to the pressure building behind Lira's eyes.

She forced herself upright. The weaver lay slumped against his stall, unconscious, silver magic smoking from his fingertips.

The shard had felled him, but spared her.

Why?

Her breath shook as she pushed back her hood. The air tasted metallic, raw with power. Something warm pulsed beneath her skin, steady and alive.

A hand clamped onto her shoulder.

Lira spun, wild instinct taking over, but it was only Kade.

Her almost-ally. Sometimes friend. Always trouble.

He looked taller than she remembered, dark hair twisted into a hurried knot, the emerald mark of the Thieves' Guild faintly glowing at his wrist. His gaze flicked from her face to her chest where the shard had struck.

"Shit, Lira," he breathed. Relief tangled with panic. "Are you hurt?"

She shook her head. "I... don't know."

"You shouldn't be here." His grip tightened. "Everyone saw that shard hit you, and everyone saw where it came from."

He had no idea how right he was.

"We need to move," Kade said. "Before the Archivists arrive. They'll be sniffing out loose magic."

Her stomach twisted. The Royal Archivists, trained from childhood to harvest and regulate memory, were feared for good reason.

They didn't ask.

They didn't listen.

They took.

"Fine," Lira whispered, letting him pull her toward the Market's shadowed edge. Her legs felt wrong, too light, too heavy, too full. She brushed her fingers over her chest. No wound, no burn. No scar. Only warmth pulsing beneath her skin.

As they fled the impact point, sound crept back into the Market, frayed, fearful. Canvas tents rippled, sigils glowing faintly: a broken quill, a mirrored mask, a hand missing a finger.

Voices chased them.

"What happened at the palace?"

"The Crown, did you see that light?"

"I felt something ancient in my head, "

Does this mean a new ruler from a different kingdom?"

"The ruler has been from Ylaria for the last three generations."

Lira kept her hood low.

Kade guided her through a narrow alley between herbalists' stalls, jars of whisper-moss trembling with captive murmurs.

"Talk to me," he said. "What did the shard do to you? Are they right, is it a Crown shard?"

Lira opened her mouth, then closed it.

If she told him the truth, he'd take her straight to the Guild. If anyone learned that she carried a relic shard worth more than the palace treasury...

Her life would never be her own again.

"I don't know," she said. "It just knocked the wind out of me."

Kade didn't believe her. He never did. "Royal shards don't just choose people," he said quietly. "They bind to bloodlines. To power."

"I don't have either."

"Exactly." His brows furrowed. "So why did it choose you?"

Heat flared behind her eyes. Lira gasped, bracing against the wall as her vision fractured.

Marble floors.

A towering throne room.

Moonlight through shattered gold.

A woman knelt in royal silk, silver hair spilling like starlight.

A shadow behind her.

A dagger.

Blood, too much blood.

Lira staggered, nearly collapsing. The vision clung to her like ice, refusing to fade.

Kade caught her. "Lira. Look at me."

But she could still smell the iron tang of blood.   The sound of steel on stone echoed in her bones. The queen's terror twisted into resignation,

Her murder, Lira thought, throat tightening. I saw her murder..

Boots thundered nearby, heavy, synchronized.

Archivists.

"We need to go," Kade said. "Now."

"Where?" she whispered.

"Anywhere but here."

They took two steps before a voice cut through the Market, cold and absolute.

"LIRA ROMAN."

They froze.

An Archivist stood at the alley's mouth, robed in violet edged with gold. The sigil at his collar shimmered, three concentric circles: memory, mind, soul.

His eyes glowed silver, an active memory-scry. "You will come with us," he said calmly. "Immediately."

Lira's blood turned to ice.

He wasn't asking.

He wasn't guessing.

He knew her name.

He knew what struck her.

He knew what she carried.

CHAPTER TWO
The Archivist's Demand

The Archivist blocked the alley with the stillness of a predator. robes whispered against the stone, their folds threaded with argent magic that shimmered and twitched, as if listening, counting the frantic rhythm of Lira's heart. The sigils stitched into the fabric pulsed once. Twice.

Kade's fingers closed around hers.

Firm. Protective. A silent vow.

"Don't speak," he breathed.

She couldn't have, even if she wanted to. Her pulse thundered against her ribs, loud enough she was certain the Archivist could hear it.

He stepped closer.

"The palace has suffered a catastrophic breach," he said calmly. Too calmly. "The Crown of Echoes has been compromised."

His gaze locked on Lira, sharp, surgical.

"We are detecting a surge of relic magic," he continued. "Localized. Recent."

A thin smile cut his face.

"From you."

Kade moved without hesitation, placing himself between them, shoulders loose, stance casual in the way of someone who had survived too many corners and too few mercies.

"She never touched the Crown," he said. "She was with me the entire time. You're mistaken."

Archivists were not accustomed to error.

The man's silver-lit irises flared. The air thickened, cold, invasive. Pressure slid into Lira's skull, prying, searching for cracks.

She gasped.

Kade's hand slipped behind him, fingers brushing the hilt of the knife hidden beneath his jacket. His knuckles grazed her hip, accidental, grounding. The contact sent a sharp warmth through her chest, anchoring her where fear threatened to scatter her apart.

The Archivist tilted his head.

"Kade," he said softly. "Orphan of the Guild. Registered dissident. Documented liar."

His smile sharpened.

"And known... selkie."

Kade froze.

The word struck like a blade.

Lira's breath caught. Selkie, a burial word. For children whose records had been erased, names scoured from ledgers by force or convenience. The Archivist hadn't merely found Kade's past.

He had excavated it.

The pressure intensified. He wanted her unsteady. Wanted her to break.

Kade's grip tightened, anger vibrating through him, and something painful bloomed beneath Lira's ribs.

"Step aside," the Archivist said. "The girl is coming with me."

Fear coiled tight in her gut. Archivists didn't interrogate, they invaded. They stripped memories from people like skin from fruit. She'd seen someone left hollow after a questioning once. A woman who couldn't remember her own name, life scraped clean.

"No," Lira said.

The word barely audible.

The Archivist stopped.

"I beg your pardon?"

She lifted her chin. Her voice steadied. "I said no."

Something shifted inside her, solid, bracing. As if the shard had grown into a second spine.

Kade shot her a sharp glance but didn't contradict her. That silence spoke louder than words.

"Very well," the Archivist said.

He rolled back his sleeve.

A metal bracer gleamed beneath, etched with ancient runes that ignited one by one.

"If you will not come willingly, "

He's going to take your mind.

The thought barely formed before the world fractured.

Lira's breath left her.

Another vision slammed into her.

Cold marble beneath her knees.

The Crown, whole, radiant, heavy with centuries of memory.

A man behind her.

A shadow.

The blade.

Pain.

Then,

A shattering. Like glass breaking across eternity.

Lira collapsed against Kade.

The Archivist staggered, eyes wide. "You're resonating with relic memory," he breathed. Hunger devoured his surprise. "Extraordinary. I will extract it now."

His arm rose.

Kade moved.

Silver energy tore through the alley as Kade dove aside, rolled, and came up behind the Archivist with the lethal grace of someone raised on survival.

"Lira!" he shouted. "Run!"

Her legs wouldn't obey.

The shard pulsed violently beneath her skin, each beat searing deeper than the last.

The air warped. Brick bowed inward.

Memories, not hers, flooded her sight.

A mother humming softly.

A boy scrambling up a tree.

A woman screaming for someone to stop.

The shard was bleeding its ghosts into her mind, and it hurt.

The Archivist spun. Kade slammed into him, driving him into the brick wall. Magic sparked against stone, scorching it black.

The Archivist snarled, striking back, his elbow cracked into Kade's ribs. Kade hit the ground hard.

"Stay down," the Archivist commanded.

Blood darkened Kade's lip as he pushed himself up.

He did not stay down.

The Archivist lifted his bracer again to strike Lira.

Desperation ripped through her, hot and blinding.

"Stop!" she cried.

The shard answered.

Light detonated from her chest, raw, uncontrolled. The force hurled the Archivist across the alley. He struck stone with a sickening crack. The runes on his bracer sputtered... and died.

The entire alley fell silent.

Kade stared at her, chest heaving, awe and fear warring in his eyes.

"Lira," he said hoarsely. "What in the seven hells was that?"

She shook her head. She had no answer.

He crossed the distance in two strides and caught her shoulders. "You're shaking." His voice was rough, but careful.

His thumb brushed her jaw as he checked her face. The touch lingered, too deliberate to ignore.

"I'm fine," she lied.

He didn't let go. His forehead dipped close to hers, not touching, but near enough that she could feel his warmth. His steadiness.

"We need to move," he said quietly.

Fear and gratitude tangled in her chest. He had fought for her without hesitation. Just as he always did.

"Thank you," she whispered.

Something unguarded crossed his face. "Always."

"Where do we go?"

Kade glanced upward, toward the rooftops where lanterns trembled like fallen stars.

"The Guild," he said. "They can hide you. For now."

The Guild was dangerous, unpredictable, loyal only when it benefited them.

But the Archivists were worse.

And the queen's dying memory still burned behind her eyes.

Lira looked at Kade.

The decision wasn't a decision at all.

"Okay," she said. "Take me there."

His fingers tightened around hers.

Together, they ran.

CHAPTER THREE
Into the Thieves' Den

Kade didn't slow until the Market of Whispers fell away behind them, until the lanterns thinned to embers and the shadows grew teeth.

Lira pressed a hand to her ribs, dragging air into lungs that refused to cooperate. Her heartbeat felt wrong. Not faster, *layered.* As if it no longer belonged to her alone.

At the market's dead end, Kade dropped into a crouch and pried loose a cobblestone worn smooth by centuries of careless feet. An iron ring winked beneath. He curled his fingers through it and pulled.

Stone shifted with the groan of something long forgotten but not dead. A narrow mouth yawned open in the ground, breathing out cold, stale air.

Lira peered into the dark. "Well," she murmured, "that's new."

"It's old," Kade said. "Just forgotten."

He tore a lantern from its post and slipped inside. Lira followed, lowering herself into the chill. The passage swallowed the light greedily, shadows closing around them as the stone slid back into place overhead.

Only then did the truth settle in her bones.

Guild territory.

The Guild of Thieves was no mere nest of cutpurses. It was an underworld kingdom, older than some crowns, answerable to none. Born of outcasts who refused to die nameless in alleyways, it had grown into a hidden empire of tunnels and safehouses, bound by codes older than the Five Realms themselves.

Here, blood meant nothing. Skill was law. Loyalty was survival.

They took in the unwanted, orphans, refugees, the unseen, and gave them what the world denied: food, shelter, training. And something rarer still.

Belonging.

But belonging had a price. To be family here, you became a thief.

It was the only reason Lira didn't join them.

Masters trained apprentices in silence and shadow, in locks that sang and illusions that bent light. They learned the Guild's codes, its ancient tongues, its hidden paths. Every initiate bore a tattoo etched with trace magic, marks that glowed faintly when the Guild was near. Kade's emerald sigil flickered at his wrist as he moved.

The Guild lived by theft, but not without law.

They did not steal from the desperate.

They did not harm children.

And they never turned on their own.

Their targets were the bloated and corrupt, nobles who bled cities dry, merchants who hoarded grain, Archivists who mistook power for divinity. To the poor, they were the Night Hands. To the crown, a nuisance. To the Archivists, a threat.

To those they sheltered, they were everything.

Torches guttered along the tunnel walls. The air smelled of damp stone and secrets that had learned patience.

Kade walked ahead, glancing back every few steps. "You're pale."

"I was almost mind-flayed," Lira muttered. "Forgive me for being a little shaken."

A short, humorless laugh escaped him. "Fair."

Silence stretched between them, taut as a drawn wire.

At last, she broke it. "Why did you help me?"

He slowed. "What do you mean?"

"You could've run. Or sold me." Her voice stayed steady. "A relic shard lodged in someone's chest would buy you half the city."

"I don't want half the city," he said.

"What do you want, then?"

He hesitated, just long enough to matter.

Then, quietly, "I want you alive."

Before she could answer, his hand closed around hers, warm and sure, and he pulled her deeper into the dark.

CHAPTER FOUR
The Thieves' Guild Does Not Welcome the Damned

The Thieves' Guild felt like the hollowed ribs of a colossal dead thing, vast, echoing, and restless with whispers that stalked the living as hungrily as a predator. As Kade led Lira through its shadow-clogged tunnels, those whispers sharpened, curling close to her skin.

Fear.

Torches guttered as they passed, flames bowing low as if in reluctant recognition. Smoke slithered upward in pale coils, serpent-thin and watchful. Every lookout stiffened at the sight of her. Not because she was armed. Not because she was powerful.

Because she was marked.

In the Guild, word traveled faster than feet.

The shard had chosen her, a royal relic of the Crown itself.

And the palace wanted her, breathing or broken, with a desperation that made even thieves uneasy.

Kade halted before a towering ironwood door, its surface carved with sigils so old they predated the Guild's first sin. He turned to her, his voice dropping.

"A warning," he murmured. "The Circle has little patience for trouble. And you..." His expression softened, just a fraction. "...you are the kind of trouble that gets people killed."

"Then why bring me here?" Lira asked.

"Because the Archivists are hunting you." He pushed the door open.

The inner chamber opened like a buried cathedral, pillars etched with stolen names, lanterns burning with witch-blue flame, a long obsidian table where the Circle of Nine waited, still and terrible, like judges who had already passed sentence.

Every gaze fixed on her.

A woman leaned forward, her hair the color of storm-washed twilight. Master Thalen, sharp as a stiletto blade's kiss and twice as lethal.

"Kade," she said, her voice smooth as drawn silk. "You arrive bearing a problem... wrapped inside another problem."

"We're asking for sanctuary," Kade said, bowing his head.

A broad-shouldered man with eyes like polished obsidian scoffed. "Sanctuary? For her?" He snapped his fingers.

A runner darted forward and dropped a scrap of parchment onto the table.

Lira's blood ran cold.

Her name.

Her face.

Stamped with the palace seal.

"A hundred gold crowns," the man said mildly. "Alive. Fifty if dead, provided the shard remains intact."

A ripple of murmurs spread through the chamber. Even thieves knew that was a fortune beyond temptation.

Kade stepped forward. "This spread too fast. It only happened hours ago."

"It's worse than you think," Thalen murmured. "It's silent. There was no posting. No record in the royal halls. Whoever wants this girl doesn't want a trial. They want her erased. So they send word to the thieves and other dregs on society"

Nine pairs of eyes bored into Lira's chest.

A thief with silver rings braided through his beard spat on the stone. "Only someone *way* up the chain can make this happen this fast and this quiet. What's rattling around in her skull that's worth more than our lives?"

Lira's pulse faltered.

She could lie.

She could flee.

She could pretend she wasn't the fracture running through the kingdom's spine.

But the queen's memory, raw and dying, pressed against her ribs.

"They murdered the queen," Lira said. Her voice barely carried. "The shard holds her death."

Silence fell, sharp as a drawn blade.

Thalen rose slowly. "You carry regicide memory."

Lira swallowed. "I carry her final breath."

The lanterns flared, then guttered. A prayer whispered. A curse answered it.

Then,

An old man stepped from the shadows.

No footstep announced him. No presence warned them. Yet when he entered the light, every thief bowed their head.

Elder Korren.

Oldest of the Guild. Oldest, some said, in the kingdom itself.

His cataract-clouded eyes fixed on Lira, and she felt him see far past flesh and bone, into places even the Archivists could not reach.

"Kade," he rasped, "why do you bring prophecy fulfilled on feet that can barely stand?"

Kade stiffened. "Prophecy?"

Korren advanced, his steps slow and inexorable. The Circle parted before him like mist.

"When the Crown is broken by sovereign hand," he intoned, "the void uncoils and seeks the land. All that was shall be devoured by the nameless void."

A shiver tore through Lira.

Korren lifted a trembling hand, hovering beside her temple.

"And the bearer of the First Shard," he whispered, "shall carry the burden."

"You knew this would happen?" Lira breathed.

"I prayed it would not." He leaned heavily on his cane. "But prophecy does not bend for our comfort."

He turned to the Circle, his voice fracturing like ancient stone.

"If the shards are not gathered,

If the Crown is not made whole,

The Unmaking will come."

Even the torches recoiled.

"Children's tales," Thalen hissed.

Korren struck his cane against the stone. The sound cracked through the chamber like thunder.

"You think this a tale?" He pointed at Lira. "She bears the Last Memory. The beginning of the end." He shook his head. "And the bounty proves the palace is already fracturing, The heir is no longer in the line of succession, The crown will choose the new king or queen once it is whole again."

Thieves muttered. Fear coiled through the room.

"Why her?" someone whispered.

Korren's gaze softened as it returned to Lira. "The Crown has its reasons," he murmured. "It is not our place to question it."

He straightened, his frail frame trembling.

"One truth remains," he said. "The bearer of the First Shard cannot outrun her fate." His eyes locked with hers. "And those who stand beside her must be prepared to lose everything."

The Circle exchanged glances, greed battling terror, ambition battling survival.

Thalen exhaled sharply. "Damn us all."

She rose. "We vote."

"On what?" the obsidian-eyed man growled.

"On whether we remember who we are," Thalen said. "We do not sell our own." She nodded toward Lira. "One of us brought her here. That makes her ours." A pause. "And on whether history will remember us as thieves, or as those who helped save the Five Kingdoms."

The words settled like a verdict.

One by one, hands rose.

Kade released a breath beside her, his fingers brushing hers, steady, grounding.

Korren bowed his head. "Then the Guild stands with either the triumphant... or the damned."

Lira didn't know whether to fall, flee, or weep.

But she knew this:

The war for the Crown had begun.

And she was no longer alone.

CHAPTER FIVE
The Hunt Begins

The council chamber emptied like sand through a cracked hourglass, leaving only the weight of Elder Korren's prophecy to thrum in the stale, subterranean air. Lira felt it press against her chest like a jagged stone, unyielding, dark, impossible to ignore.

Kade lingered at her side, one hand hovering near the hilt of his blade, a sentinel poised to strike down fate itself if it dared move. Even in silence, his presence steadied her.

Elder Korren unfolded an ancient parchment, the ink shimmered faintly, as though alive, murmuring secrets only the world remembered.

"We have precious little time," the elder said, voice a gravelly whisper. "The shards of the crown must be reunited before the Devouring Dawn. To do so, you must first recover a relic capable of revealing their hidden resting places."

Lira's lips trembled as she wet them. "Where?"

The elder's gaze darkened, cold as ice. "The Wraithmere Ruins."

A shiver rippled through the chamber like a living thing. Everyone knew the name. The cursed labyrinth where no flame burned true, where magic faltered, and walls whispered until travelers wandered willingly into death.

Wraithmere lay deep within the kingdom of Thalen, carved from black stone long before the five kingdoms were united under a single crown. No living soul knew its builders, some whispered of an ancient order of Precogs. Others insist the ruins were raised by the gods themselves.

But all agree on one certainty: Wraithmere existed to test those who sought forbidden power.

Inside lies a vast and shifting maze, walls that rearrange themselves, corridors that loop back on impossible angles, and pathways that vanish behind those who walk them.

The deeper one ventured, the louder the ruins whispered. Voices slid through the stone, seductive siren murmurs, tempting travelers with the cadence of their own memories, their fears, their desires. Many vanished, lured into traps by the sound of a loved one calling their name.

The ruins are littered with dangers: pressure wards that trigger spears of light, illusion pits that swallow travelers whole; only a handful in each generation ever make it to the heart of Wraithmere.

At the center chamber, upon a pedestal of onyx, rests the Seer's Eye. A relic of old magic, the Seer's Eye is said to grant its bearer the ability to find whatever they seek, lost truths, lost memories, buried secrets, even the scattered shards of the Crown of Echoes.

"You can't be serious," someone muttered.

"I am," Korren said. "Lira must retrieve the Seer's Eye if she is to find the pieces in time."

Before she could protest, Kade stepped forward. "Then she will have protection." His voice carried no hesitation, no fear. It made Lira's heart falter.

Korren inclined his head. "Good. But one blade will not be enough." He scanned the chamber. "Three volunteers."

A hush fell. One by one, the Guild's finest stepped forward, Kade's closest friends.

Tamsin, wiry and sharp, a wicked grin and always ready for mischief. Bren, the massive enforcer with a bloodied past and unexpectedly loyal core.

Evo, the shadow of the Guild, a tracker who sees everything and is rarely seen- until it is too late.

They pressed hands to heart, bowing not to her, but to the cause.

"For the Shards," Tamsin said.

"For the realm," Bren intoned.

"For the girl who can save it," Evo murmured.

Lira swallowed hard. Kade's hand brushed her shoulder, barely there, but enough to remind her she wasn't alone.

"There is more you must know," Korren said.

The lanterns dimmed as he approached her, pressing two cold fingertips to her temple. Shadows writhed. Her breath caught.

"When the Shard awakens," he whispered, "its magic burns through its bearer. It gives, yes... but it also takes."

Lira shivered. "Takes what?"

"Pieces of yourself. Memories. Time. Each use of its power erodes the person you are."

Kade's jaw tightened. "And you're telling her this now?"

"There is no kindness in ignorance," Korren said. "Only despair."

Before she could reply, a shrill whistle split the air.

Everyone froze.

"That's the outer perimeter alarm," Tamsin said. "Someone's found the Guild."

A violent explosion shook the chamber. Dust rained down from the ceiling.

Bren snarled. "Blasted magic. They want someone dead."

Another boom. A support column cracked.

Jace's panicked voice echoed from the stairwell. "Strike team! At least twelve hunters, they're breaking through the south wall!"

Kade's stance sharpened, precise as a drawn blade. He reached for Lira, pulling her closer. The others grabbed their evac-bags; packed for quick escapes.

"Stay behind me." He said, grabbing his bag from Tamsin, eyes burning with unspoken promise.

The southern wall erupted. Armored hunters stormed through, quick and silent and terrifyingly efficient. Their commander lifted a gauntleted hand and pointed directly at her.

"Seize the Shard bearer. Kill the rest."

Thieves clashed with hunters, slowing them down, steel ringing against steel. Lanterns shattered in the storm of chaos.

Korren shoved a leather satchel into Lira's hands. "Maps to Wraithmere. Supplies. Leave, now."

"But the Guild, "

"Will survive if you do," Korren cut her off. "Go!"

Kade grabbed her hand, dragging her behind a crumbling pillar. Bren barreled through enemies like a living battering ram. Tamsin's knives flew with surgical precision. Evo melted into the shadows, already flanking the intruders.

Kade's voice was calm, lethal. "We don't win this fight. We escape it."

Tamsin appeared beside them. "West tunnels are still open, but not for long."

"Let's move," Kade commanded.

"On your mark," Tamsin said. She had a wicked smile and almost seemed excited for the action.

His eyes met Lira's, dark, unyielding. "I'm not losing you," he whispered.

Then,

"Mark," he said firmly.

And with that, the Guild erupted into chaos, fleeing into shadow, racing toward the first step of destiny.

CHAPTER SIX
Wraithmere Ruins

The tunnels swallowed them whole, a cavernous maw of darkness.

Kade led the way, Lira close at his side, Tamsin, Bren, and Evo forming a tight, protective shield around them. Behind them, the echoes of fighting dwindled, fading into silence, or perhaps being swallowed by the Guild itself.

The Guild was either winning... or buying them time with blood.

Lira forced herself not to glance back.

"Keep moving," Kade murmured, his voice steady despite the adrenaline scorching through them. "They'll take you alive, but they won't let you live."

Tamsin struck a torch alight. The flame sputtered, shivering like a caged spirit, but held.

"Tunnel forks up ahead," Evo whispered, voice barely audible.

"Too many choices," Lira panted, breath hitching in the damp air.

"Not if you know the thieves' markings," Tamsin said, a sly smirk curving her lips. She traced faint scratches along the stone, low by the floor, spirals for danger, X's for dead ends, arrows for safe exits.

"These tunnels... are mapped?" Lira blinked, incredulous.

"Thieves go everywhere," Bren snorted. "Even where we shouldn't."

A distant boom shook the earth, rattling dust from above.

Kade squeezed her hand briefly, instinctive, protective, then let go.

"Run."

They did.

The tunnels twisted, rose, dropped, and split, but Tamsin's markings guided them true. At last, a cold breeze brushed their faces.

Evo crept forward, peering through a narrow opening. "Surface. Sun's gone down."

"Better for us," Kade said. "Harder for the hunters."

Harder, Lira thought, but not impossible.

They emerged onto a rocky hillside, moonlight illuminating a forest below. And beyond, the horizon revealed their destination: A desolate sprawl of stone, draped in shadow. The Wraithmere Ruins.

Lira felt her stomach knot. "We really have to go there."

Bren cracked his neck, as if reading the same grim prophecy. "Prophecies usually mean yes."

"Comforting," Tamsin muttered sarcastically under her breath.

They descended cautiously, keeping a steady pace to put distance between themselves and the hunters.

The stone paths of the Ruins chilled them to the bone. The air was unnervingly still.

The moment they crossed the first fallen archway, Tamsin's torch sputtered violently, then died.

"So much for that," she muttered, shaking it.

"Try mine," Bren offered. His torch flared briefly, then dimmed to a struggling ember.

"It's the place," Evo whispered, eyes scanning the darkness. "It eats light."

"And magic," Lira breathed, reaching inward, searching for even the faintest pulse of her Shard's power.

Nothing.

As though the Ruins themselves had wrapped fingers around her power and squeezed.

Kade watched her, jaw tight. "Don't force it. Not here."

"But if we need, "

"We'll manage without," he said softly. "You're not losing pieces of yourself in this maze."

Tamsin cleared her throat loudly. "So! Maze, death whispers, no magic, torches that barely work. Fun."

They pressed deeper.

The corridors shifted subtly, blocks shifting under their feet, hallways twisting just a little between breaths. Evo walked at angles, eyes darting to walls like he expected them to lean in and swallow him whole.

"They're moving," Lira whispered.

"No," Evo corrected. "They want us to think that. Trick of perspective. Clever, though."

"Clever how?" Bren asked.

Evo pointed to a tiny carving near the floor: a faint Guild mark. "Others made it this far. Left messages."

The etching read: **DON'T TRUST THE SHADOWS. THEY LIE.**

Lira swallowed hard. "Great."

They followed the low, cryptic markings, as if the walls themselves had been designed to distract from anything at eye level.

After twenty minutes, whispers began, faint at first, then forming words.

Lira jerked, heart hammering.

The walls whispered in her mother's voice: *Lira... turn back... you were never meant to survive this...*

Her breath caught.

Kade slid in front of her. "Don't listen."

The whispers twisted around them. Tamsin heard her dead brother's laugh. Bren heard desperate, pleading voices. Evo's eyes flickered, unreadable. Kade heard nothing.

The walls didn't speak his language of fear.

Lira tried to shake her head, but the voice sweetened, seductive: *Kade doesn't trust you. He'll abandon you. He knows what you are, useless,*

"Enough!" she snapped, pressing her palms to her ears.

"That's exactly what it wants," Evo hissed. "It wants us to stop thinking. Wants us emotional. Stupid. Distracted."

Tamsin smirked. "Wrong room for that."

They pressed on, ignoring the whispers, while Tamsin left her own secret markings along the stone floor and lower walls.

Bren halted, pointing ahead. "Shimmer, the artifact maybe?"

Lira peered past him.

A soft, cerulean glow pulsed at the end of a spiraling hall.

The artifact rested on a stone pedestal: a crystalline orb etched with faint runes.

The Seer's Eye.

Older than the Crown of Echoes itself, if the legends are to be believed. It was created by a precognitive warlock known as The First Seer, a man said to see every thread of fate at once.

According to ancient lore, the Seer foresaw a future where kings, queens, and conquerors would spill oceans of blood to claim his power. To prevent that fate, he tore out his own gifted sight, his third eye, and forged it into a crystal sphere of living magic.

But he knew hiding it would not be enough.

So he carried the relic into Thalen and carved the Wraithmere Ruins with his own hands.

He, bound the Eye to the ruins with by one immutable law: only the worthy may touch it.

All others would be claimed by the Ruins.

"The tool that can find the Shards," Lira whispered.

"Careful," Kade murmured.

Bren reached toward it. The orb flickered, dimmed, then flared. He froze.

Tamsin held her breath. Evo crouched, scanning the floor for traps.

"There," he said. "Trap."

"What kind?" Bren asked.

"The lethal kind. Looks like pressure plates. If we move wrong, the Eye could..." Evo stopped, frowning. "Actually, I'm not sure. But I'm sure it won't be good." He murmured.

The walls whispered louder, whispers overlapping, desperate, hungry.

Kade steadied Lira with a touch on her arm but looked toward the others, "We're thieves. Think like thieves. How do we take something old, possibly cursed, and magically aware?"

Tamsin grinned. "Same as any heist. Distract it."

Bren cracked his knuckles. "Hit it?"

Evo sighed. "No, you baboon. *Subtle* distraction."

Lira blinked. "Subtle how?"

Evo motioned to the floor. "Watch the dust pattern. Anything moving too quickly shifts weight. We need... a decoy, and balance."

Tamsin drew a small mirror from her satchel. "Reflective light. Not real light, just enough to confuse it."

Kade handed it to Lira. "On my mark, shine the mirror toward the Eye. Evo, be ready to grab the orb. Bren, hold him steady if the floor starts shifting."

"And me?" Tamsin asked.

"Try not to die," Kade said.

She winked. "Always the plan."

Kade shook his head, "Just be ready... we're the balance."

Lira angled the mirror.

"Now."

A thin beam of faint moonlight slipped in from a crack in the ceiling, hitting the mirror, reflecting across the chamber, bouncing sharply across the stone. The Eye flickered, uncertain.

Evo darted forward and slid his hand beneath it, lifting it in one fluid motion. Easier than expected.

The pedestal remained still. Three tense seconds passed.

Then,

The Seer's Eye glowed steadily in Evo's palm. "We have it," he whispered. In the eye he saw an image of Lira appear. When he handed Lira the eye, it flared just for a moment.

Lira exhaled in relief just as the whispers died. The silence that followed was worse than the noise.

Kade's gaze shot upward. "Not good."

The maze rumbled ominously.

"Time to leave," Bren urged.

"Fast," Tamsin added.

"Very fast," Evo corrected.

Kade clasped Lira's hand and together, they ran.

CHAPTER SEVEN
The Labyrinth Wakes

The moment they burst from the chamber, the maze itself groaned, a deep, ancient sound like a beast waking from a long sleep.

The stone walls shuddered.

Floors trembled beneath their boots.

Kade's fingers tightened around Lira's hand. "Don't look back. Just run."

But the labyrinth had no intention of letting them leave unscathed.

Evo skidded to a halt at the first fork, chest heaving, eyes darting between three twisting corridors. "Left was right on the way in," he said, breathing hard. "But the maze, "

THUNK.

A massive stone wall slammed into place behind them, sealing off the chamber they had barely escaped.

Bren swore, voice sharp. "We pick a path now, or die here."

Tamsin crouched, scanning faint Guild carvings etched near the floor. "This one. Move!"

They lunged left, just as the floor behind them cracked open, revealing a chasm of swirling black mist.

"Not dying today," Bren growled, shoving Tamsin forward.

The corridor twisted sharply, and then, the whispers returned.

But these were no ordinary illusions. These were warnings: *You should not be here. Give it back. Give it back, or be swallowed.*

Lira stumbled, knees buckling under the weight of the voices. Kade caught her, arm circling her waist. "Lira, look at me."

Her breath caught. "It's inside my skull... tearing my thoughts apart,
"

"I've got you," he said, voice low, fierce, grounding. "Stay with me. Focus on my voice."

The maze roared, an explosion of sound.

Stones ground together. The walls on either side began inching inward.

"We're going to be crushed!" Tamsin snapped. "Move!"

She sprinted through the opening.

Evo flung himself down the narrowing corridor. Bren shoved at the walls with raw strength, giving Kade and Lira the precious seconds they needed to slip through. Kade never let go of Lira as he pulled her forward.

The walls slammed shut behind them.

"We can't outrun it forever," Lira panted. "It's reacting to the Eye. It wants it."

"It can want the eye," Kade said. "But it's not getting you."

Ahead, a faint orange glow flickered, torchlight, but not theirs.

Tamsin stiffened. "We're not alone."

Evo moved first, silent as smoke, peering around the next turn. He pressed himself back to the wall, expression grim. "The strike team. They followed us."

"How?" Bren demanded.

"They couldn't have traced our path," Evo said.

Kade clicked his blades softly, a sound like sharpening teeth. "They know we came for the artifact. They need it to find the shards."

Lira's pulse slammed against her ribs. "How many?"

"Eight. Elite. Moving in formation," Evo said.

"We can't fight in here," Tamsin hissed. "One misstep, one wrong swing, and we trigger another collapse."

Lira clutched the Seer's Eye to her chest. "Then... what do we do?"

All eyes turned to Kade. He scanned the twisting, shifting walls, listening to the rising whispers as if reading the maze's intentions.

"This maze wants to confuse," he said. "So we turn that to our advantage. We make it our ally."

Tamsin's grin was sharp and wicked. "Thief trickery. I like it."

Kade pointed to faint Guild symbols etched low on the walls. "These markers, they don't have to mark safe paths alone. Some can lead to false trails on purpose, design them to confuse. Let the strike team follow them straight into the maze's teeth."

"And since the palace knows nothing of thieves' codes..." Tamsin finished, "they'll stumble right into our trap."

Evo nodded. "Perfect."

Bren crossed his arms. "All we have to do is avoid the traps ourselves." He exhaled dryly. "Piece of cake."

Kade turned to Lira. "You trust us?"

She blinked. "Of course."

A fraction of a smile softened his face. "Stay close. No matter what. If I say stop, you stop. If I say move, you move. Understand?"

"Yes." Her voice barely more than a whisper.

He grasped her hand again, this time deliberately. "Good."

They moved, silent, swift, methodical.

Evo left false footprints in dust. Tamsin carved misleading Guild sigils at eye height. Bren hefted massive stones to simulate collapsed tunnels. Kade led Lira along the true, narrow path.

Behind them, the strike team entered.

Seconds later, a scream echoed. Another. Then a thunderous crash as part of the maze collapsed upon itself.

"One down," Tamsin whistled.

"More like three," Bren said, grinning.

Evo raised a hand. "Not all. Two are close."

Lira pressed the Eye to her chest. Ahead, the corridor opened into a cavernous exit, the only way out. Torchlight flickered behind them.

Kade swore under his breath. "They're faster than I expected he muttered.

"Then we run," Lira said, surprising herself with the steel in her voice. Kade's eyes widened, pride flickering, then he nodded.

They sprinted. Dust exploded with each stride as blades struck Stone beside them. Two hunters burst into the chamber, movements lethal.

Bren met the first with a roar, slamming into him like a battering ram.

Tamsin darted forward, slashing the second's, legs and vanishing before he could retaliate.

Evo slipped behind him, slicing his hamstrings with surgical precision.

"Kade, !" Lira shouted as a crossbow rose.

Kade spun, knocking the weapon upward; the bolt embedded in the ceiling. He drove an elbow into the hunter's throat, he crumpled.

The chamber shook. The maze screamed in protest, furious that its prey was escaping with the Eye.

"Go!" Kade shouted.

Lira bolted for the exit arch as the floor split behind her. Kade caught her around the waist, leaping with her across a yawning chasm. They landed hard on the other side as the floor collapsed behind them.

Bren and the others barreled through an instant later, leaping the great distance.

The stone arch slammed shut like a massive jaw.

Then,

Silence.

They were outside. Breathing, alive. And still clutching the Seer's Eye.

Kade exhaled slowly, brushing Lira's for the briefest moment.

"We're safe," he whispered.

Behind them, the ruins rumbled, one last, ominous warning.

45

CHAPTER EIGHT
The Eye Opens

The moonless night pressed cold and sharp against their skin as they tumbled from the labyrinthine ruin, collapsing onto jagged stones beyond the reach of Wraithmere's cursed walls. Lira clutched the relic, the Eye, against her chest, its weight more than metal and stone, a pulse of ancient hunger against her palms.

Kade kept an arm braced around her shoulders, steadying her wobbling form. Sweat streaked the dirt across his temple, but his eyes swept the barren terrain like a predator born to vigilance, always watchful, always protective.

"You're shaking," he murmured, voice a quiet anchor.

"It's not me," she whispered, "it's this thing."

Evo flung himself onto a boulder, chest heaving. "Whatever curse that maze was built on... I never want to see it again."

Tamsin rubbed at her ears as though trying to scrub away the lingering whispers. "I still hear the walls calling names that weren't mine."

Bren cracked his knuckles, the sound loud in the quiet night. "If they whisper again, I'll punch that maze in the face."

Kade exhaled a tired, almost amused breath. "You can try."

But Lira barely heard them. The Eye throbbed in her palms, slow and relentless, like a heartbeat carved from stone.

"We need to know what it can tell us," she breathed.

"Better here than in there," Evo muttered, nodding toward the ruins.

Kade met her gaze. "All right. Let's see what it shows us."

She swallowed hard and lifted the relic. The carved eyelid remained half-shut, the obsidian surface reflecting only their dark shapes under the starless sky.

"It reacted to you in the chamber," Tamsin said, stepping closer.

"Maybe it needs, " Lira didn't finish. The Eye answered for her.

A gasp tore from her throat. Light flared from the carved eyelids, cold, blinding, fierce, spilling across their faces like frostfire. Evo shielded his eyes. "By the gods, !"

Bren cursed and staggered back.

Tamsin gripped Evo's sleeve, grounding herself against the strange brilliance.

Kade stayed by Lira, hand steady on her arm. "I've got you," he said, not as command, not as assumption, but as certainty.

Then the Eye opened fully.

The night vanished. The ground fell away beneath them. Wind screamed past their ears, though none of them moved not a hair's breadth. The world shifted.

They stood on cracked earth under a blood-red dawn. A desert stretched endlessly, Cracked earth splintered in all directions, and far across the wasteland rose a jagged cliff of black stone. Atop it, crumbling but defiant, leaned a solitary spire, a broken watchtower, a sentinel dying yet unbowed.

Tamsin whispered, "Emberwatch Spire."

Lightning arced behind it, white and jagged, frozen in the sky. The storm behind the tower did not move. It hung suspended, like a thought half-formed.

The desert ground before the tower rippled. First like wind over sand, then darkened, twisted. Something massive stirred beneath the dunes, a shadow coiling, circling its prey, unseen but certain.

The Eye drew them closer, until the spire loomed overhead. Fallen stones cracked apart to reveal a barrier of wild, living magic, pulsing with a heartbeat of its own, sending sand shivering with every thrum.

And then, snap.

They stumbled back into the night outside Wraithmere. The Eye's glow dimmed, though warmth lingered against Lira's palms. Silence pressed heavy around them.

Bren exhaled. "So... that's where the next piece is."

"And whatever storm that is..." Evo muttered, "...doesn't look good."

Tamsin crouched beside Lira, fingers brushing the ground. "I thought it was only guiding her... but it showed all of us."

Kade's gaze sharpened. "Yes. Because she holds it."

Evo nodded. "I held it in the chamber. A moment." His jaw tightened. "It only showed me a flicker of her. Lira. A trail back to her shard."

Lira's breath hitched. "It... tracks me?"

"No," Tamsin said, tilting her head. "It tracks the shard, the closest shard."

"That's the same thing right now," Evo said.

Kade stepped closer, voice low and certain. "The Eye knows you carry a piece of the Crown. It responds. It seeks all the pieces."

Lira swallowed. "So if any of you hold it..."

"It brings us right back to you, the closest shard," Bren said. "Convenient, in case we lose you."

Kade shot him a look. "We won't."

Heat pricked Lira's cheeks despite the cold night.

Evo wiped dust from his hands. "But when *you* hold it, it reveals the next closest shard. That vision was a map."

"A warning," Tamsin corrected. "Nothing that ominous comes without danger."

Kade rested a hand on the hilt of his blade. "Then we head for Emberwatch Spire at first light."

Lira clutched the Eye tighter. Its faint pulse synced with her heartbeat.

She wasn't royal. She wasn't trained. She was a stray, a shadow in the world's gaze. And yet, this ancient power had chosen her, and the others had chosen to follow.

Kade met her eyes, firelight from their makeshift camp reflecting in his. "You're not alone in this, Lira."

Warmth unfurled in her chest, quiet, dangerous, hopeful.

She nodded. "Then tomorrow," she whispered, "the real hunt begins."

CHAPTER NINE
The Road of Red Sand

They left Wraithmere behind before dawn, slipping away at the first gray smear of morning. At last, Kade said the words they were all waiting for: "Move. The longer we linger, the more this place remembers us."

Lira kept the Eye wrapped in cloth, cradled close to her ribs. Even muffled, its faint pulse throbbed against her skin, steady, insistent, alive.

As the sun climbed, the broken wilderness of Wraithmere gave way to the Red Frontier, a barren expanse of cracked earth and rust-colored sand, stretching endlessly until the desert swallowed the horizon.

Bren marched ahead, cleaving a path through jagged stone when necessary. Tamsin's eyes flickered constantly over the dunes, scanning for movement, shadows, anything out of place. Evo trailed beside Lira, unnervingly silent, every so often crouching to inspect a footprint or a scattered bone.

Kade, however... Kade stayed near her.

Not pressing, never smothering. But always there. Always watching with that quiet, lethal focus that made danger seem just a step behind but never quite upon them.

"You're limping," he said as they climbed a slope of red stone.

Lira jolted. "Am not."

"Lira," he murmured, gentle, but unyielding.

She scowled at the ground. "Maybe a little."

He shifted closer, offering support without touch, the simple nearness of him grounding her. "Let me see."

"No." She spoke lightly, but her voice betrayed hesitation.

His brow arched. "Humor me."

Her foot throbbed, bruised from a misstep in Wraithmere's collapsing labyrinth. She held out her ankle without meeting his gaze.

Kade crouched, hands careful on her boot. "You should have said something."

"You had bigger things to worry about than my foot," she muttered.

He paused. "Your safety... is never a small thing."

A strange warmth rose up her spine. Unfamiliar, unwelcome in the best way. She did not pull away.

Evo's voice cut through, sharp and distant. "Tracks ahead."

Kade stood immediately, The warrior-mask slid back over Kade's face. "Human?"

"Maybe," Evo said, crouching to study the careful tread, the boots' light step. "Someone who knows how to hide, but not as clever as they think."

Tamsin knelt beside him, tracing her fingers over the red sand. "Could be scavengers."

"Or palace scouts," Bren growled.

Lira tightened her hold on the Eye. "Do you think they're close?"

Kade didn't answer. He didn't need to.

They pressed forward.

By midday, the desert unfolded like a living thing, rolling dunes shimmering in heat, the air tasted metallic, every breath felt stolen, heavy with sun-baked dust.

And yet, the desert was not empty.

The wind made a sound thin and high like distant laughter.

Tamsin froze. "That... isn't wind."

"What is it?" Lira whispered.

"Sand sirens," Evo said, voice low. "They mimic voices. Travelers follow them, walk into ravines or sinkholes. Sometimes they never return."

Bren's jaw tightened. "Or they follow the sound until they collapse, and the sirens take whatever's left behind."

A shiver ran through Lira. The siren-voices shifted, whispers curling like smoke, faint giggles, a voice eerily like her own calling her name. Instinctively, her hand curled around Kade's sleeve.

He did not look at her. Did not comment. He only shifted closer and said, "Listen only to us. They're scavengers, so they won't attack physically, they pick apart the dead, not the living."

They fell into a tight formation, Kade at her side, Bren ahead, Evo and Tamsin covering the rear. The laughter followed them, fading only when the sun began to sink.

By evening, they reached a field of broken red stone, the first sign they neared Emberwatch territory in the kingdom of Oranth. Veins of black iron ran like scars through the earth.

Lira stepped onto a jagged slab, and the Eye pulsed violently against her ribs, shaking her spine.

Kade's hand went to the hilt of his sword. "The relic?"

"Yes," she breathed, unwrapping just enough to reveal its faint glow. "It's reacting. We're close."

"How close?" Evo asked, tilting his head.

She hesitated. "I... don't know."

The Eye pulsed again, tugging like invisible fingers, pointing toward distant dunes.

Tamsin followed Lira's gaze. "It's leading the way."

Kade stepped close enough that their shoulders brushed. "Don't force it. Pain is a warning. Respect it."

She shook her head. "It doesn't hurt. It wants us to go there."

Bren looked uncomfortable. "That's not reassuring."

They camped in a shallow ravine as the twin moons rose pale and thin over endless sand, the desert wind curling like cold fingers around them. A small fire flickered, throwing light over worn, tense faces.

Lira sat at the edge, knees drawn close. Kade approached quietly. "Can I sit?"

She nodded.

He settled beside her, careful not to crowd, and for long minutes, they watched the moons climb.

Finally, Kade said, "You did well today."

She huffed a breath.

"You kept a good pace, even when you were hurting," he continued.

Lira looked down at her hands. "I'm not like you," she murmured. "Or Tamsin. Or Evo. Or Bren. I'm not trained. Not brave."

His voice dropped to a whisper, almost lost in the wind.

"Lira... you survived alone. In a world that tried to crush you. That takes more strength than any sword I've ever held."

Her breath caught.

"You're stronger than you know," he said, eyes soft. "And whether you realize it or not, this shard chose wisely."

Heat flushed her cheeks, but she didn't look away.

For a heartbeat, it seemed as if he might reach for her hand.

Then Bren snored loudly on the far side of camp. The moment shattered.

Kade rose, offering a small, tired smile. "Try to sleep. We move at dawn."

She watched him return to the others, heart hammering. She had promised herself long ago never to need anyone.

But she did.

CHAPTER TEN
The Storm That Watches

The desert changed with each mile they crossed.

At first, jagged spires of stone clawed skyward, ancient and unforgiving, like the ribcage of some long-dead beast. But now the land softened into rolling waves of red sand, each dune rising and falling like the breath of a slumbering giant. The air itself tasted wrong, metallic, electric, humming with a tension that gnawed at the edges of their minds.

Evo was the first to notice. He dropped to one knee, palm pressed flat against the sand. "The ground... it's moving."

Bren snorted. "From what? We're in the middle of nowhere."

"No," Evo said slowly, brushing sand from his fingers. "Something beneath us is moving."

Tamsin stiffened. "Burrowers?"

"Too big," Evo murmured.

Lira's hand tightened around the Eye beneath her cloak. Every few minutes it pulsed, harder, sharper, as if invisible claws tugged at it from somewhere ahead. Her chest shivered in sympathy.

Kade stepped closer, his gaze slicing through the heat haze. "Is it the Eye?"

"Yes," she whispered, voice trembling. "But my shard... it reacts too."

She pressed her hand to her sternum. Beneath skin and bone, the sliver of Crown metal embedded there, usually dormant, blazed now, slow waves of heat radiating outward. Not yet painful, but unnerving in its intensity.

Kade's jaw tightened. "Stay close."

The words might have irritated another, but for Lira they were a lifeline, steadying her shaking hands.

By mid-afternoon, they reached the base of a dune so colossal it swallowed half the sky. Red sand spilled down its flanks in molten rivers, each grain catching the sun like sparks from a forge.

Bren shaded his eyes. "We're going up that?"

"The Eye points that way," Lira said.

"Then up we go," Kade decided, already striding forward.

Halfway up the slope, the shard within Lira's chest flared, vibrating against her ribs. She gasped and stumbled.

Kade was there in an instant, arm firm around her waist. "Lira?"

"It's... vibrating," she hissed. "Something's wrong."

Evo spun on his heel, eyes scanning the shifting sands. "Something's under the sand."

The dune trembled.

Then it moved.

A low groan rolled through the ground, resonant and immense, shaking through Lira's bones.

Tamsin's eyes widened. "That's not the dune... that's, "

Then the sand erupted.

A serpent of impossible scale, armored in jagged plates of earthen stone, its red scales glinting like fire in sunlight, burst skyward. Its body was thick as a ship's mast, its head crowned with obsidian horns carved sharp as blades.

A red-scaled sand viper. Very rare, legendary and lethal, towered above them, casting a shadow that swallowed the slope.

Bren whispered, horrified. "Oh... we're dead."

The creature hissed, a sound like grinding storms of sand and stone. Kade shoved Lira behind him, sword drawn. "Move back!"

Evo and Tamsin flanked them, weapons ready, faces pale but resolute.

Lira clutched the Eye, feeling the carvings bite into her palms. The relic pulsed with desperate urgency, thrumming in tandem with the shard in her chest. She lifted it, gazing into its depths, and saw it.

Not with her eyes, but through the Eye itself.

A pulse of light stabbed out, illuminating the serpent's massive chest. For a single, shivering breath, she saw through the scales, into the creature's heart.

And there it was. A shard. Another piece of the Crown, beating like a second heart inside the monster.

"It's inside it," she choked.

Tamsin risked a glance. "Inside... what?"

"The shard!" Lira's voice trembled. "It's in its heart!"

Bren blinked. "In its heart?"

Kade cursed softly. "The Eye didn't show a storm, it showed the desert swirling around something powerful. We thought it was a storm."

Evo's nod was grim. "It wasn't metaphor. It was interpretation."

Tamsin shook her head. "A serpent guarding the shard... makes more sense than a storm holding it."

The shard in Lira's chest pulsed again, sharper now, echoing the serpent's movements.

"It feels like it's calling to it," she whispered.

The beast lunged.

Kade yanked Lira aside as sand erupted around them. Evo rolled down the slope and sprang back up with a dagger in hand. Tamsin darting left, eyes scanning for weaknesses. Bren roared and hurled a boulder down the dune, striking the serpent's head, but only drawing its attention.

"We need a plan!" Tamsin shouted.

"I've got one," Evo said, eyes hard. "Don't die."

"That's your plan?" Bren bellowed.

"It's a starting point!" Evo snapped.

The serpent reared, its throat glowing faintly like molten fire building within.

Kade grabbed Lira's shoulders, forcing her to meet his gaze. "Tell me what the Eye showed you. Tell me what you feel."

"I... I think it wants us to get the shard," she stammered. "But it's fused inside the serpent. I don't know how to take it out."

Kade's voice softened, steady as iron. "Then we find a way together."

Her heart pounded against her ribs.

"We are getting that shard," he said, eyes blazing. "And we are getting out alive."

The serpent's roar tore across the desert. The sand quaked beneath them. The shard in Lira's chest flared like a living sun.

And Kade raised his sword. Every line of his body spoke a single truth: the storm the Eye had shown them was not wind. It was this. A guardian. A monster. A challenge. And it was watching them now.

CHAPTER ELEVEN
Heart of the Beast

The serpent struck again.

Sand exploded upward in a violent plume as its horned head slammed into the ground where Lira had stood only seconds before. Kade yanked her backward behind a jagged ridge of stone, his breath harsh as his eyes swept the battlefield with a soldier's sharp focus.

"Everyone in one piece?" he called.

"Define *piece*," Evo muttered from the left as he crouched behind a broken slab, shaking sand from his hair.

"I think I lost a tooth," Bren groaned.

"You did not," Tamsin said, wiping grit from her daggers. "You'd be screaming much louder."

"I can start," Bren offered.

"No," Kade snapped, not unkindly, just focused. "Be quiet. It senses its prey through vibration."

Lira pressed a hand to her racing heart. The shard buried in her chest pulsed like a second heartbeat, wild and erratic, answering the creature that carried its twin. Each throb sent a lance of heat across her ribs, stealing her breath.

"I have to use the Eye," she whispered, her voice unsteady. "Along with the shard's power."

Kade turned sharply toward her. "The shard?"

She nodded. "I have to get close. Mine is calling to the one inside it. I don't know if I can stop it once it starts."

"You won't have to," he said. "We'll get you close enough to end this quickly."

Bren snorted. "Close enough? To *that* thing?"

Evo peered around the stone just in time to see the serpent's massive coils grinding through the sand like shifting hills. "It's circling," he said. "Hunting in arcs. Locking onto the strongest signal."

Tamsin lifted her dagger and pointed it toward Lira. "Her."

Lira swallowed. "I know."

"Then we use it," Kade said.

Tamsin blinked. "Use... Lira?"

Kade looked directly at her, not through her, not past her. "Only if she agrees."

The Eye throbbed in Lira's grip. Her chest burned, and fear coiled tightly in her gut, alive and watching. She hesitated only a moment before nodding.

"I'll do it."

Kade released a slow, steady breath. "Good. Here's the plan." He knelt and drew rough lines in the sand. "Bren hits from the left and draws its focus. Evo goes high and targets the eyes. Tamsin gets onto its back. Those plates are thick, but there will be seams."

Tamsin grinned. "I love seams."

"I'll stay with Lira," Kade continued. "I'll get her to the heart."

Bren stared at him. "Close? Kade, you saw its chest. That thing is armored."

"Not everywhere," Kade said. "When it rears to strike, the underside splits. That's our opening."

Lira swallowed again. "And what exactly am I supposed to do?"

"You use the Eye," Kade said. "Like you said you would."

She flinched. "I don't know how. I don't have an instruction manual."

"Then we improvise," he replied. "You aim it."

"Aim it?" Evo echoed. "Like a weapon?"

"No," Kade said. "Like a key."

The shard inside Lira's chest pulsed harder, sharper, pain blooming beneath her sternum.

"A key to what?" she whispered.

"You saw into the serpent's heart before," Kade said. "Do it again. Push deeper. If the Eye can reveal the shard, maybe it can weaken the bond, or give your shard something to pull against."

"And if it doesn't?" she asked.

"Then we adapt," Kade said.

Bren muttered, "Great. Improvising while being eaten."

Evo elbowed him. "Shut up."

Tamsin rolled her shoulders. "I'm ready."

Kade turned back to Lira. "You stay with me. You don't leave my side. Understand?"

"Yes," she said, her throat tight.

He touched the back of her hand, not reassurance, but resolve. "Together."

The serpent struck first.

Bren charged with a roar, swinging his full weight behind a jagged boulder and slamming it into the serpent's jaw. The beast recoiled, its massive head snapping toward him, fanged maw gaping wide.

From the ridge above, Evo launched himself into the air, hurling dagger after dagger into exposed flesh. The blades skidded and sparked against the creature's armored hide, failing to pierce, but the distraction was enough.

"Tamsin, go!" Evo shouted.

She became a blur of leather and steel, sprinting across the serpent's coiling body. She leapt from scale to scale, boots finding impossible footing, before driving a hooked blade deep into its spine and anchoring herself in place.

"I'm in position!" she shouted.

"Kade," Lira breathed, clutching the Eye as its weight burned against her palms.

"Now," he said.

They ran.

Heat rolled off the serpent in crushing waves, stealing breath and blistering skin. Kade dragged her beneath the creature's rising head as it reared back, its chest swelling, molten plates shifting and grinding against one another.

"LIRA!" he shouted. "NOW!"

She lifted the Eye.

It pulsed, harder than ever before, and the world tore away from her.

Light swallowed her vision.

Heat filled her lungs and seared through her veins,

Then everything snapped back into focus.

She could see inside the serpent.

Her body still stood beside Kade, but her sight, her senses, her very essence were pulled into the labyrinth of the creature's heart. It beat slowly, powerfully, ancient beyond reckoning, formed of molten stone and living fire.

And within it,

The shard.

It was fused deep within the heart like an anchor, bound by veins of metal and blazing heat. Lira gasped as the Eye burned against her palms.

Pull it free.

The whisper did not reach her ears. It spoke directly into her mind.

How? she thought desperately.

The shard embedded in her own chest pulsed in response, hard, urgent, demanding. Her shard was answering the call, reaching toward its twin.

Kade's voice broke through the distance, strained and fading in and out.

"Lira, come back, LIRA, "

She forced her eyes open.

The serpent had reared high above them, its chest fully exposed, molten, massive, and throbbing with terrible power. Kade was holding her upright, his arm locked tightly around her waist, keeping her from collapsing.

"Tell me what to do," he said.

"I can free it," she whispered. "But I have to use my shard too. They're connected. I need to link them."

He went utterly still. "Will it hurt you?"

"I don't know," she admitted. "But I have to try."

She swallowed hard. "I just need you to hold me steady."

"Done," he breathed.

And she believed him.

Lira pressed the Eye to her chest, directly over the shard beneath her skin.

The desert roared.

The serpent roared back.

And Lira reached for the heart of the beast.

A shockwave tore outward, ripping through the sands. The ground convulsed as spirals of sand and fire hurled into the sky.

The serpent screamed, an earsplitting, metallic shriek that split the heavens.

Kade braced his feet and hauled her against him as the world shook violently beneath them.

"Lira, what's happening?!"

She couldn't answer.

The Eye's light blazed white-hot, flooding her body. Every nerve ignited. The shard in her chest surged, burning, relentless. It no longer reacted to the serpent's shard. It was pulling it.

"Move!" Kade shouted.

Bren, Evo, and Tamsin dove behind jagged stone outcroppings as the serpent's throat swelled with molten light. The creature bucked violently, fighting against the force tearing at its heart.

"I can't, hold, " Lira choked, her legs collapsing beneath her.

Kade dropped to one knee beside her, wrapping both arms around her torso and anchoring her as the air screamed with raw energy. "I've got you. Stay with me."

The Eye lifted from her hands, its carved iris rotating as if alive. A beam of searing gold light burst from Lira's chest and slammed into the serpent.

The impact cracked like thunder. Armored plates splintered. Scaled hide peeled away. The monstrous heart was laid bare, molten, blazing, crowned by the shard buried deep within.

"THERE!" Tamsin shouted from the ridge. "LIRA, NOW!"

The serpent's head snapped toward them, jaws widening, ready to swallow them whole.

Kade shouted over the roar, gripping her tighter. "Lira, now!"

She reached out, not with her hands, but with the Eye, pushing her mind outward. "Come to me," she whispered.

The shard embedded in the serpent's heart flared. Then it tore free.

The serpent's scream shook the earth as the shard ripped itself from living flesh, tearing through molten bone and erupting from its chest in a violent spray of fire and light. The creature convulsed, its massive body buckling as the magic abandoned it.

The shard shot straight toward Lira. Kade tightened his grip, bracing her, and bracing himself.

The impact was brutal. A burst of blinding energy slammed into her sternum like a meteor. Her breath vanished. Her body jolted backward, every nerve ablaze. She would have collapsed if Kade had not held her.

The shard did not deflect. It sank into her, through skin, through bone, to the place where the first shard already lived. Two shards. One born in her chest. One torn from the serpent.

Lira screamed. Light exploded outward, a shockwave flattening the sand for thirty feet in every direction. The serpent collapsed with a final, broken convulsion, its molten heart dimming, then extinguishing entirely.

Kade held her as she trembled violently. "Lira, LIRA, look at me!"

Her back arched, fingers clawing into his shoulders as fire surged through her veins. Inside her chest, the shards fused, melting together in a searing blaze of heat and power that felt far too vast for her body to contain.

Her heartbeat faltered. Stopped. Then thundered back to life. Two pulses. Two shards. One shared rhythm.

Kade pressed her face to his chest, one hand cradling her head. "Come back," he whispered fiercely. "I've got you. Come back to me."

The light faded slowly. Lira sagged against him, breath shuddering, her skin pale and faintly luminous from within.

"I... I have it," she whispered, her voice barely holding together.

Kade let out a sound that was half breath, half broken relief, pulling her closer. His forehead rested against her temple. "You scared the hell out of me."

Evo approached cautiously, eyes wide. "Is she... alive?"

"I'm alive," Lira murmured, her words barely more than a whisper carried on the desert wind.

Tamsin slid down the dune, her chest heaving. "Did it work?"

Lira lifted a trembling hand to her chest. Her skin glowed softly, no scar, no wound, only a faint golden light radiating from beneath the surface.

"I have two shards now," she said, her voice fragile but steady. "They... fused."

Bren stared at her in disbelief. "Inside you?"

She nodded, clutching Kade's tunic as if letting go might undo everything.

"And it didn't kill you?" Evo asked, his voice tight with concern.

"It..." Her breath hitched. "It almost did."

Kade growled softly, not at her, but at the cruel world that demanded such a price.

Tamsin brushed sweat-slick hair from her face and let out a shaky laugh. "Well. That's one way to beat a monster."

Bren kicked the serpent's still-twitching tail. "That thing isn't coming back, right?"

"No," Lira said quietly, her gaze lingering on the lifeless form. "I took its heart."

The desert fell silent.

The serpent was dead.

The shard was theirs.

And Lira, small, homeless, forgotten Lira, now carried two pieces of the Crown embedded within her chest.

Kade looked at her, something fierce and fearful burning in his eyes. "We're getting you out of this desert," he said softly. "Before anything else tries to claim you."

"That would be good," she breathed.

"The Eye has to tell us where to go next. Are you all right to hold it?" Tamsin asked, the concern in her voice just barely masked.

"I can do it." Lira tried to rise, swaying, and Kade was there instantly, steadying her without a word.

She turned the Eye over in her hands and waited. When it opened, the glow was faint, weak, almost hesitant.

"I think it needs time to recharge," Evo said.

"No... look." Bren pointed.

The vision brightened, sharpening with startling clarity. The Spire of Embers filled the Eye's sight, no shifting sands, no cryptic symbols. Only the spire itself, standing tall and imperious, and a basin of black stone at its base.

"Does that mean there's still a shard there?" Bren asked, squinting at the image.

"I don't think so..." Lira tilted her head, listening to something only she could feel, a hum beneath her skin. "But we still have to go. The Eye wants us to see something there."

CHAPTER TWELVE
The Spire of Embers

The desert finally broke.

Endless waves of red sand gave way to black volcanic stone, cracked and steaming beneath the late-afternoon sun. Emberwatch Spire rose from the northern cliffs of Thalen like a burning fang, tall, narrow, and veined with fissures that glowed faintly even in daylight. It had once been the secluded home of the precognitive warlock known as the First Seer, the same enigmatic figure who had created, and hidden, the Seer's Eye.

Built centuries before the five kingdoms were united, the Spire had been carved directly from volcanic rock. Its walls hummed with dormant sigils, ancient wards shimmering faintly beneath layers of dust and time. No one knew how long the Seer had lived there, only that he withdrew from the world to refine his magic, believing that true foresight required absolute solitude.

Then, one day, he vanished.

His disappearance left the Spire abandoned, but not empty.

Travelers who approached Emberwatch at night claimed the cracks in its stone pulsed with molten light, as if fire moved behind the walls. Scholars dismissed it as residual magic, but the people of Thalen whispered a different truth:

The First Seer had never truly left.

His spirit still flowed through the Spire.

And the walls remembered his visions.

Lira felt the fused shards humming inside her chest, warm and steady. Not painful. Not chaotic. She recovered faster than she should have. Strength filled her, deeper and surer than anything she had known before. It was not borrowed. It was not fleeting. It felt earned.

Kade noticed it, the certainty in her stride, the way her breath no longer caught after the climb.

"That glow in your chest," he said quietly, "it's getting brighter."

"It feels... good," she admitted. "Like I'm finally more than the things that happened to me."

He offered one of his rare, soft half-smiles. "You always were."

Her heart skipped, but before she could answer, Evo raised a fist, signaling them to stop.

"We've got a problem," he murmured.

From the cracked ridge ahead, a gust of cold wind surged outward, unnatural, cutting. The air turned brittle. Fog spilled across the rocks, hissing where it met the heat.

Tamsin shivered. "That's not weather."

"No," Lira whispered, every hair on her arms lifting. "Something is, "

A wail tore through the air.

Not human.

Not beast.

Wraith.

A giant one.

It erupted from the fog like a nightmare dragged through a tear in the world, nearly twenty feet tall, a swirling mass of smoke and bone. Its face stretched long and hollow, shadow dripping from it like tar.

It shrieked, and its empty gaze locked onto Lira.

"BACK!" Kade shouted, already pulling her behind him.

The wraith lunged, its massive hand clawing toward her.

Bren charged first, slamming both fists into the creature's wrist. The impact sent a shockwave through the ground, scattering shards of rock as the wraith reeled back with an inhuman screech.

Tamsin sprinted up a boulder, launched herself into the air, and slashed through the wraith's smoky tendons. Her blade cut cleanly through, its arm buckled, form flickering as it struggled to hold shape.

Evo moved like a shadow, twin curved daggers carving into the creature's legs. Each strike sent fragments of the wraith scattering like wind-torn ash, but it reformed instantly.

"It wants Lira!" Evo shouted. "Badly!"

Kade planted himself in front of her, sword blazing with reflected light. "It's not getting her."

The wraith lunged again, faster this time.

Kade met its strike head-on. Sparks flew as metal clashed with spectral bone. He pivoted sharply and sliced through its ribs, and the creature shrieked, stumbling backward.

Bren seized the opening. While the wraith was still solid, he lifted a massive fallen slab of obsidian and slammed it down onto its skull with brutal force.

The wraith's head shattered, then reformed, snarling.

"It won't stay down!" Bren roared. "It won't stay solid!"

Lira clutched her chest as the shards inside her pulsed, fast and urgent.

"Kade," she gasped, "I feel something. It's like the shards are... warning me."

"Then stay behind me," he said, voice firm and unwavering.

The wraith shrieked again, its voice climbing to a pitch that made the surrounding rocks tremble. Shadowy tendrils lashed toward Lira like whips of black lightning, slicing through the air with a hiss.

Kade spun, looping an arm around her waist and pulling her flush to him as the tendrils slammed into the ground where she had been standing. Stone split, sand scorched, and the echo of impact rattled the cliffs.

"Keep moving!" he shouted, dragging her forward with every ounce of strength.

The group closed ranks around Lira, forming a defensive circle. Bren planted himself at the front, bracing for impact. Kade guarded her flank with precision. Tamsin slashed at every strand of shadow that dared to reach too close, while Evo struck silently and swiftly beneath the creature's sweeping blows.

Use the power of the shards.

The thought came to Lira, soft and urgent, almost as if it were not entirely her own. She lifted one trembling hand, and a surge of raw energy rose from deep within her.

Golden light erupted around her, forming a dome of pure shard energy that shimmered and blazed with overwhelming brilliance. The wraith's claws struck the shield and burned away like smoke curling from embers. The creature shrieked and recoiled, unaccustomed to such force.

Kade stared at her, stunned. "You, Lira. You did that?"

"I think," she said, breathless, "I can do more."

She stepped out from behind him, ignoring his sharp protest.

"Lira, wait, "

But she did not stop. Both hands rose toward the wraith. Inside her chest, the shards flared, two hearts beating as one, thrumming to her command.

A golden pulse exploded outward from her, striking the creature's core with a force that made the earth beneath them tremble. The wraith convulsed, screamed, and began to unravel, its smoky form tearing apart thread by thread. It lashed out one final time.

"Leave us!" Lira shouted, her voice carrying across the stones like thunder.

The wraith burst into ash and vanished. Silence fell, thick and suffocating.

Kade lowered his sword slowly, awe in his eyes. "Remind me," he said faintly, "never to get on your bad side."

She managed a tired, unsteady smile. "You never will," she whispered.

But then her body went rigid. The shards inside her chest pulsed, once. Twice. And the world dissolved around her.

She found herself standing in a throne room, once grand but now draped in shadow. A queen lay dying on the marble floor, blood pooling beneath her. Her crown, whole and shimmering, still rested atop her head.

Bent over her was a man. His face was mostly hidden beneath a palace guard's helm, but the smile he gave, cold and serpentine, cut through the vision like a knife. He pressed a dagger to the queen's throat and whispered, "For the Wraith King."

The queen struggled for breath. With her last strength, she tore the crown from her head. Her hands shook violently as she smashed it against the stone, sending shards scattering across the room in a burst of light.

The man snarled, rage flashing in his eyes. The queen collapsed, and the vision shattered.

Lira's knees buckled beneath her as she returned to the desert, the shards inside her still glowing faintly. Kade caught her instantly, gripping her shoulders.

"Lira, talk to me. What did you see?" he demanded.

Her voice trembled as she fought to steady her breath. "The queen," she said. "I saw the moment she died."

Tamsin stepped closer, brow furrowed. "How?"

Lira lifted a trembling hand and pressed it against her glowing chest. "The shards showed me," she said.

Evo narrowed his eyes. "What else did you see?"

She swallowed hard before speaking. "There was a man. He was dressed as a palace guard, but he wasn't one."

Kade's jaw tightened. "Who was he?"

"I, I don't know," she whispered. "I've never seen him before."

Bren let out a low grunt. "Then what happened?"

A chill spread across Lira's skin. "He killed her," she said softly. "And right before she shattered the Crown, he said, "

Her voice cracked, trembling.

"'For the Wraith King.'"

The group froze, the weight of Lira's words hanging heavy in the air. Kade's expression hardened, his eyes narrowing into dangerous slits. "Then this is no longer just a betrayal within the palace," he said, his voice low and steely, each word carrying the threat of retribution.

Lira lifted her gaze to the glowing Spire looming in the distance, its light cutting through the darkness like a warning. "And the Wraith King," she said, her voice trembling but resolute, "he wants the shards. Every last one of them."

Beneath her skin, the shards throbbed, pulsing with a light that seemed to echo her fear and determination. They reacted as if aware of the danger that now hunted them all.

CHAPTER THIRTEEN
Echoes in the Spire

Emberwatch Spire loomed like a broken needle driven into the desert's scorched horizon. Its once-gleaming stone was cracked and veined with ember-red light, as though fire still breathed beneath its skin. Behind them, the giant wraith's smoke thinned on the wind, fading like a nightmare that refused to fully release its hold on her.

Lira pressed her palm against her chest and felt the fused shards pulse beneath her skin. Two pieces now, woven together as if they had always been meant to reunite. Strength hummed through her, hotter than blood and steadier than breath.

She did not feel unstable.

She felt right.

Kade, however, watched her as though he remained unconvinced.

"Still with us?" he murmured. Sand clung to the edge of his jaw, and dark residue dripped from his sword, remnants of the wraith they had slain only minutes earlier.

Lira managed a crooked smirk. "You think a giant killer wraith out for my blood can scare me off?"

"It's not the wraith that worries me." His gaze dropped briefly to her chest, to where the crown's fragments slept beneath her skin. "It's you using the shards' power, and the cost that comes with it."

Evo's voice lowered. "The elder warned her, didn't he?" He hesitated, his expression softening. "That every time she draws on the shards' power, she loses pieces of herself."

Silence settled heavily among them.

Lira swallowed. The truth cut through her newfound strength like a blade.

Yes, the elder had warned her.

Yes, she felt stronger than she ever had before.

Yes, the shards felt right inside her.

But something had shifted all the same. She simply did not know which part of herself was missing.

Boots crunched against stone as Bren brushed dust from his arms with a grunt. "We're wasting daylight standing around. If there's another monster hiding in that tower, I'd rather break its skull before the sun goes down."

Evo snorted. "You just want something to punch that isn't made of sand and smoke."

Tamsin already had her blades in hand. She tipped her chin toward the towering entrance. "Argue later. The Spire's waiting."

They moved on.

The air changed the moment they crossed the threshold. It grew colder and heavier, threaded with the faint scent of roses long dead. Emberwatch's interior spiraled inward, its hallways warped and fractured, murals peeling from the walls in ghostly fragments. Ash clung to every surface.

As they descended deeper, whispers stirred in the darkness, brushing past Lira's ear like a breath.

Lira... Lira...

She stiffened.

Kade immediately stepped closer. "What did you hear?"

"Nothing," she said, lying without hesitation.

Because the voice had sounded like the queen.

The same queen whose vision had revealed the treacherous guard.

The same queen who had shattered the crown with her dying breath.

The Eye tugged faintly from the pouch at her hip, vibrating with a low hum. It wanted something. It recognized a place it had once ruled.

They turned a corner, and a narrow chamber opened before them. The space was lit only by a pale ember-red glow seeping from cracks in the stone. At the far wall stood a basin of blackened crystal, half-melted by ancient fire.

Carved above it were words, half crumbled but still legible.

THE PATH APPEARS ONLY FOR THOSE WHO SEE.

Tamsin let out a low whistle. "Well, that's about as clear as mud."

Evo folded his arms. "It probably means we need the Eye. The warlock who forged it lived here."

Lira reached for the relic and stepped toward the basin.

The moment the Eye drew close, heat flared through her palm. Mist gathered above the basin, shaping itself into words that lingered just long enough to be read before swirling away.

THE CROWN MUST BECOME WHOLE AND BE TAKEN TO THE ROYAL PEAKS.

THERE THE NEW LINE OF SUCCESSION WILL BE MADE KNOWN.

SEE THE PRIESTESS OF THE ROYAL PEAKS AND TAKE A COMPLETE CROWN.

Then everything changed.

The fused shards in Lira's chest flared gold and red, filling the chamber with a trembling hum. The Eye snapped open.

A sandstorm erupted.

A mountain of black glass rose toward the sky.

A buried vault glowed with frost.

A shattered bridge stretched over endless mist.

A hand, her hand, reached for a third shard.

Then a location burned into their minds with crystal clarity.

THE FROSTMADE VAULT.

THE SHARD BURIED IN ICE THAT NEVER MELTS.

BEYOND THE SPINE OF WINTER.

The vision shattered with a sound like splintering bone. The Eye slammed shut.

Evo exhaled sharply. "That's a lot of information, and it's very far north."

"Past the civilized maps," Tamsin added.

Bren crossed his arms. "At least now we know where the crown needs to go when this insane mission is over."

Kade ignored them. His focus never left Lira. "Are you all right?"

She nodded slowly, though her pulse still thrummed with strange heat. The shards felt restless after the vision, unsettled by what they had seen.

"I'm fine," she said. "And we know where to go next."

As they turned to leave, the whisper returned, clearer now, echoing inside her mind.

The queen's voice.

"Hurry, child. The Wraith King moves faster than you think."

Lira froze.

Kade's hand brushed against hers. "Lira?"

She forced a steady breath. "We need to move. Now."

CHAPTER FOURTEEN
The Frostmade Road

The sun hung low over Emberwatch Spire by the time they stepped back into the open air. Its heat had softened to a dull, copper glow. The desert stretched before them, quiet and empty, deceptively peaceful. The wraith's ashes had already vanished into the wind.

Lira inhaled deeply, letting the warmth steady her. The echo of the queen's whisper still clung to her bones.

Kade did not move forward with the others.

"Walk with me," he murmured.

Evo raised a brow but said nothing. Tamsin smirked knowingly, as if she had already guessed his intent. Bren only shrugged, as though he had expected this moment.

Lira rolled her eyes at them, then followed Kade toward a jagged outcrop overlooking the dunes.

They stood in rare silence. It pressed heavily between them, thick enough to make speaking feel dangerous.

Kade stared out over the sand, his jaw tight. "The shards, the Eye, all of it keeps pulling us deeper into danger."

"You can still walk away," Lira teased gently, though her voice wavered.

"That is the one thing I cannot do." He turned to her, eyes blazing.

Warmth flared in her chest. Some of it was her own, and some came from the shards responding to his nearness.

Then his gaze dropped to the faint pulse beneath her skin.

"What did it feel like?" he asked quietly. "When the Eye showed us that vision?"

She hesitated. The truth felt too intimate to speak aloud.

"Like being opened," she whispered. "Not broken, just exposed. It feels as if the shards know me better than I know myself."

Kade swallowed hard. "That's what worries me."

"Kade, "

He reached out and brushed his knuckles along her cheekbone. The touch was so gentle it nearly unraveled her.

"I am afraid of what this crown might be shaping you into," he said. "I am afraid of what it might take from you."

The elder's warning echoed in her mind: every use of the shards' power would steal pieces of her.

Lira forced herself to meet his eyes. "I am still me."

"For now." His hand fell away, though it remained close. "Just promise me you will let me help, whatever comes next."

She swallowed hard. "I will."

She meant it.

When they rejoined the group, Bren was sharpening his axe against a slab of stone. Evo and Tamsin crouched over a rough map drawn in the sand.

Evo traced a northern route with his finger. "The Frostmade Vault lies beyond the Spine of Winter. We can either cross the northern gorge or circle around the basalt cliffs."

"Circling adds two weeks," Tamsin said.

"And the gorge is crawling with ice wraiths," Bren added cheerfully. "I like the gorge."

Lira crouched beside them. "We take the gorge. The vision showed jagged cliffs and frost, not flat plains."

"And visions never lie?" Tamsin asked.

"They lie only when people misread them," Lira replied. "This one was clear."

"All the more reason to move tonight," Evo said. "The palace is close."

He was right.

Kade scanned the horizon, his hand resting on his sword. "Speaking of that, "

Movement flickered across the dunes.

Then more followed.

Riders appeared.

Armored, fast, and silent.

Palace hunters.

Lira's breath caught. "They tracked us."

"No," Evo said, narrowing his eyes. "They were watching us, waiting."

The hunters spread into formation, dust rising behind them. Their armor reflected the dying sun like shards of a shattered mirror.

The lead rider raised a hand, and the others took aim.

"Down!" Kade shouted, grabbing Lira and pulling her aside.

Hooked chains tore through the air.

Bren swung his axe in a wide arc, slicing two chains apart mid-flight. Tamsin spun, knives flashing, pinning another chain to the sand. Evo dropped low and rolled beneath a second volley.

Kade held Lira close as a chain snapped through the space she had just occupied.

"They are trying to take you alive," he growled.

"Not if we ruin their day first," she replied, breathless.

The palace hunters vaulted from their mounts in perfect unison. Their sand-silk cloaks moved as one, and their narrow visors gave no hint of expression.

It was the same uniform the queen's killer had worn in Lira's vision.

One hunter lunged. Kade met him with steel and fury.

Bren intercepted two attackers at once, slamming one into the sand hard enough to make the ground tremble. Tamsin weaved between blades, cutting straps and slashing tendons. Evo vanished into the dust and reappeared behind a hunter, twisting his arm until it snapped.

Lira fought too, but in a different way.

The shards burned beneath her skin, urging her to unleash them.

The elder's warning echoed again: pieces of herself.

She clenched her fists.

No. Not yet.

Instead, she reached for the Eye without fully opening it. She let its awareness brush her thoughts.

Paths unfolded before her. Weak points in armor. Shifts in the sand. Perfect angles of attack.

She slipped between two blades, ducked under a third, and pivoted, driving her elbow into a hunter's throat.

He collapsed, gasping.

She stepped back, stunned by what she had done.

As their formation broke, the remaining hunters retreated with chilling discipline. They mounted their steeds within seconds and vanished into the dunes, as if they had never been there.

Dust settled.

Silence followed.

Kade wiped his blade clean. "They were not trying to kill us."

"No," Lira said, her pulse still racing. "They were testing us, or trying to capture me."

"Or measuring how close they can get," Tamsin said, sheathing her knives.

Bren spat into the sand. "Let them come closer next time."

"It does not matter why they came," Evo said. "They left empty-handed."

Lira's jaw tightened. There was no reason to delay further.

"We leave now," she said. "The Spine of Winter lies deep in Veskain territory."

Kade stepped to her side, his gaze steady. "We are with you."

The desert wind rose, swirling sand around their boots.

Together, they began the long march toward the frozen lands.

CHAPTER FIFTEEN
The Spine of Winter

The heat of the desert had faded long before they reached the foothills.

By the second day of traveling north, the red dunes gave way to stretches of cracked earth, veined with frost. The air thinned, sharpened, carrying the metallic tang of snow yet to fall.

Tamsin shivered dramatically. "Wonderful. I've always wanted to freeze to death slowly."

"You won't," Bren said, adjusting the pack on his shoulder. "You'll freeze fast. Quick and merciful."

"That is not better," she shot back, glaring at him.

Kade snorted under his breath, and Lira bit the inside of her cheek to keep from smiling.

For the first time since Emberwatch, the tension among them had lifted, just enough to allow teasing. Just enough to breathe.

The cracked ground soon gave way to a narrow valley carved between colossal slabs of stone. Wind howled down the passage like something alive, threading between jagged towers of basalt dusted in cold ash.

Lira hugged her cloak tighter. "Feels like the mountains are... watching."

"They are," Evo said dryly. "But that's normal for the Spine."

"How comforting," she muttered.

"It is comforting," he insisted. "Means we're on the right path."

"That's not... how comfort works, Evo," Tamsin said.

"Maybe you're just too soft for northern travel," he shot back.

She flicked a pebble at him without looking. It hit him squarely in the forehead.

Kade made a strangled noise that might have been a laugh.

By nightfall, they found shelter beneath a stone overhang, where someone long ago had carved crude runes marking it as a resting point for travelers.

Bren gathered fallen branches, brittle and dry. Kade coaxed the fire to life. Tamsin set a kettle of melted frost to boil. Evo sharpened his blades with meticulous care.

Lira sat nearest the flames, letting their warmth seep into her frozen fingers.

It wasn't long before Tamsin nudged her with a smirk. "You ever think about how weird we are?"

"Weird?" Lira asked.

"Four thieves, a cursed crown, and a girl with glowing ribs. That's weird."

Bren barked a laugh. "We're not weird. We're just... uniquely unfortunate."

"Speak for yourselves," Evo said, polishing his blade. "I'm incredibly fortunate."

Tamsin rolled her eyes. "You grew up stealing boots off sleeping drunks at the docks. How fortunate could you possibly be?"

"Very," Evo said smugly. "I learned early that drunk men don't chase you if they don't have boots."

Kade shook his head, smiling despite himself. "He's not wrong."

Lira glanced at him. "What about you? How did you end up in the Guild?"

Kade paused, the sharpening stone hovering above his blade. Sparks fell, then stilled.

"I was... found," he said at last. "I was a kid running messages for smugglers, picking fights with anyone who looked at me wrong."

Tamsin snorted. "Some things never change."

He shot her a withering look but continued. "The Guild gave me direction. It gave me a place to put all the things I used to throw at the world."

Evo smirked. "And we still have to keep him from burning himself out."

Kade ignored him and turned back to Lira. "What about you? How did you survive before all this?"

The fire cracked once, then settled into an uneasy hush.

Lira worried the edge of her cloak between her fingers. "I did not have anyone. No parents. No home. I sold memories at the Market of Whispers just to buy enough food to keep from collapsing."

Tamsin's expression softened. "Selling memories, Lira, that's., "

"I know," Lira said quietly. "But when you're starving, it doesn't matter what you lose. Only what keeps you alive."

Bren scratched his chin. "That's a hard way to grow up."

"Harder to keep going afterward," Evo murmured.

Lira smiled, small and almost shy. "The Guild didn't owe me anything. I wasn't one of you, and I still am not. But you helped me anyway. You protected me. I... didn't expect that."

Kade met her gaze across the fire, his expression steady and warm.

"You're one of us now."

Her chest tightened in a way that had nothing to do with the cold.

She cleared her throat. "Does anyone know anything about the Frostmade Vault?"

They exchanged glances.

"I only know that it exists," Tamsin said with a shrug.

The others nodded in agreement.

"Well... that's reassuring." Bren remarked sarcastically.

Later that night, while the others got ready for bed, Evo slipped quietly to the ridge overlooking their camp. Lira noticed and followed him.

"You're restless," she said softly.

"So are you." He tilted his head toward the valley below. "There," he said. "Third shadow past the ridge. Do you see it?"

She narrowed her eyes.

A flicker.

A low-moving shape.

A rider.

Her pulse quickened. "Palace hunters?"

"Two," Evo murmured. "And another farther south. They've been with us since Emberwatch."

Her stomach tightened. "Why haven't they attacked again?"

"That's the strange part," Evo said. "They are staying far enough to watch us and close enough not to lose us. But they're not pushing."

"Waiting?" she whispered.

"It feels like it," he replied. "Attacking us has not worked out for them so far."

Tamsin appeared beside them without a sound, making Lira flinch. "Thieves three, hunters zero, last I checked. If they wanted her dead, they would have struck already."

"They want something else," Evo said.

Bren joined them with a grunt. "They're waiting until she has all the shards."

Lira went still.

Behind them, Kade stepped into the firelight, his face half-shadowed.

"Then we make sure they never get the chance," he said.

His eyes met hers, fierce and unyielding, a promise forged in iron.

She nodded as the cold wind tugged at her hair.

Because whatever the palace hunters wanted, whatever the shards were shaping her into, and whatever waited within the Frostmade Vault, they would face it together.

CHAPTER SIXTEEN
The Gorge of Wraith Ice

The wind in the Spine shifted as the mountains gave way to something colder, sharper, as if the land itself were sharpening its teeth. By the time the team reached the edge of the Gorge of Wraith Ice, snow swirled in ghostlike threads, clinging to their clothes and biting any skin left exposed. The gorge stretched before them, a mile-wide chasm of jagged blue crystal and ancient fissures, glowing from within as if lit by trapped souls.

Kade blew into his hands, breath pluming in the frigid air.

"Every time I think we've found the coldest place in the realm," he muttered, "the world finds a way to prove me wrong."

Evo gave him a faint grin. "You're lucky you still have fingers to complain with."

Bren stepped forward to study the rim. "The bridge we're looking for should be natural ice. Strong enough, if the winds stay low."

Lira said nothing. Her gaze drifted across the gorge, its unnatural sheen, its dizzying depth, its faint, humming resonance. The Eye pulsed in her chest like a heartbeat, stirring again, sensing something hidden.

They moved single-file along the narrow ridge that curved perilously over the steep drop. The path was barely wide enough for a boot, and snow had gathered in uneven drifts, masking slick frost beneath.

Lira pressed a gloved hand to the rock wall to steady herself. Behind her, Evo's voice drifted forward, calm but measured.

"Watch the surface. The wind carves pockets; it won't hold everywhere."

"I wasn't planning on falling," she called back.

"No one plans on it," Evo said, and Bren snorted.

Kade flashed Lira an exaggerated grin, cheeks flushed from the cold. "If one of us falls, Lira will just reach out with shard magic and float us to safety."

Lira rolled her eyes. "That's not how it works."

"Well," Evo said from behind her, "let's try to avoid putting it to the test."

They crossed the first narrow shelf without incident. The second required carefully navigating around a jut of ice that had grown over the gorge like a frozen claw. Lira edged around it cautiously.

Evo followed, but the moment he shifted his weight, the snow beneath him gave a brittle crack.

"Evo, wait, !" Lira warned, but it was already too late.

The entire ledge beneath him sheared off in one clean break. Evo's foot slipped. His body lurched sideways. Snow exploded into the air. And then he was gone, over the edge.

Lira didn't think. She moved.

She dove flat onto the ridge, one hand digging into the rock as she flung the other toward the abyss. Her fingers closed around Evo's wrist, a jarring, skin-burning impact.

His weight yanked her forward with such force that a sharp cry tore from her throat.

Evo dangled over a sheer drop of hundreds of feet, snow swirling around him in a frenzied vortex of white. His other arm flailed, searching desperately for something to hold.

"Lira, !" he gasped, boots kicking at nothing but air. "Don't let go!"

"I wasn't planning on it!" Her voice cracked, strained by effort, as her shoulder flared with searing pain.

Her gloves slipped against his bracers. She tightened her grip, nails biting through the leather.

"Bren!" she shouted. "Kade!"

"I'm coming!" Bren's heavy boots thundered across the ridge.

The ledge beneath Lira shifted, a whisper of movement, but it was enough to shoot terror through her spine. Evo felt it too, his grip tightening instinctively.

"Don't move," she whispered.

"I'm just going to hang out here for a while," he said through clenched teeth, attempting humor, failing miserably.

Kade slid into view first, crawling carefully to distribute his weight. His face was pale, lips nearly blue from the cold.

"Pulling her will collapse the whole shelf," he muttered, eyes scanning the spiderweb cracks radiating from Lira's precarious perch.

Bren dropped beside him, urging Kade to shift. "We can anchor. Lira, hold him steady."

"Working on it," she hissed, fingers burning from the strain.

Tamsin kept her distance, not wanting to add to the weight.

Bren braced his boots against a higher rock formation and grasped Kade's forearm. Together, they locked themselves in place like living supports.

"Lira, on my count," Bren said. "Shift his arm up toward me. Slowly."

Lira nodded sharply, the fear choking her breath in her chest.

"Three... two... one."

She dragged Evo's arm upward. The movement nearly yanked her over the edge; her boots skidded against the ice, desperately seeking purchase. Kade's hand reached out, fingertips brushing Evo's sleeve.

"Got him, just a bit more!"

Lira gritted her teeth and heaved. Pain lanced through her shoulder and down her spine, but Evo's arm rose. She didn't know how she managed it, adrenaline, sheer will, or both, but somehow, she kept him from plummeting.

Kade latched on fully, securing Evo's arm at last.

Then Bren hauled back with a guttural shout.

Evo scrambled upward, not gracefully, not easily, but with a desperate, scraping frenzy, as Bren and Kade dragged him onto the ridge.

Lira collapsed against the snow, chest heaving, limbs trembling from exertion. Flakes drifted around them, soft and silent, settling like fragile witnesses to their struggle.

Evo rolled onto his back, gasping for breath. After a long moment, he turned his head toward Lira.

"You good?" he asked, voice ragged.

"No," she rasped. "You?"

"Not even close," he huffed.

Kade, wide-eyed and pale, let out a shaky laugh. "Can we... not do that again?"

Bren made sure Evo was fully on stable rock before lowering himself onto his heels. "Next time you see a patch of snow that looks 'a little off,' don't test its integrity with your entire weight," he warned.

Evo groaned. "Noted."

Only then did Lira realize how violently her body was still shaking. Evo pushed himself upright, wincing as he moved. Slowly, deliberately, he reached out and rested a hand on her arm.

"Thank you," he said quietly, each word heavy with sincerity.

Lira swallowed hard. "I couldn't just let you fall."

"You didn't hesitate." His gaze held hers, steady and sharp, carrying a weight that made the air between them tense and electric. "That means something."

Kade clapped his gloved hands together, breaking the charged moment. "Right. If the gorge could stop trying to kill us for at least the next ten minutes, that'd be great."

Above them, the wind rose in a hollow, mournful howl.

The team gathered themselves again, bruised, shaken, breathing hard, but alive.

Tamsin patted Evo on the back. "Glad you're not dead."

"Aww, you do love me." He replied while dramatically batting his eyelashes at her.

She rolled her eyes. "Whatever." Somewhere deep below, the icy glow pulsed once more, as if the gorge had merely been testing them.

By the time they recovered from Evo's near-fall, the snow had thickened into a drifting haze. The team pressed on along the narrowing ridge, each shaken in their own way, even Bren, though he masked it behind his stoic silence. The wind screamed through the teeth of the gorge, biting their faces raw and stealing warmth from their bones.

Ahead, carved into the far side of the chasm, lay their destination: the Frostmade Vault.

It appeared first as flickers of strange blue light, rippling through the snowstorm. Then the shape solidified, an enormous circular door sculpted into the cliff face, etched with runic seams that glowed like captured lightning. Massive pillars of ancient ice framed the entrance, each humming with a faint, eerie resonance that made the hair on Lira's arms stand on end.

Kade exhaled, awe breaking through his fear. "That... is a vault. Big enough to keep a god trapped in it."

"Or a shard shaped by one," Bren murmured, eyes narrowing at the intricate runes.

The Eye pulsed against Lira's chest as if responding to the ancient structure, a quiet, rhythmic tug that pulled at her very core. The shard she had absorbed shifted faintly, pulling toward the vault, as though it were calling to something hidden within.

Lira stepped forward, but Evo caught her by the elbow.

"Let us scout first," he said softly, still shaken, but steady enough to lead.

She nodded, though her gaze remained fixed on the runes, older and more ancient than anything she had ever seen.

They descended the final, narrow stair of ice, carved by centuries of frost and wear. At the bottom lay a plateau, flat and wide, leading directly to the vault's towering door. The temperature dropped the instant they stepped onto the frozen ground, so bitter it seemed to ring in their teeth.

"Feels like walking into a frozen lung," Kade muttered, his breath puffing out in frantic white plumes.

The runes brightened as they approached, their glow sinking into Lira's skin like invisible threads. Her fingertips tingled.

Bren crouched near the door, gloved fingers tracing the carvings. "These markings predate the Queen's rule. Older than any spire texts."

Lira swallowed. "It was built to guard something."

Evo's gaze swept over the ridges above. "No palace hunters. Yet."

"Yet," Kade echoed, his voice low and dark.

Lira stepped closer to the vault.

The Eye flared, hot and cold at once, sending a shock straight through her bones. A faint crackling sound rippled across the ice.

"Lira," Evo warned, "don't touch, "

But the vault responded before she could.

The runes erupted to life, flaring from deep blue to blinding white. Snow burst outward in a swirling ring, and the humming intensified until the very air vibrated like struck metal.

A seam split down the center of the circular door.

"Oh, good," Kade muttered weakly. "It's opening by itself. That's not terrifying at all."

With a grinding groan that echoed through the gorge, the Frostmade Vault opened.

Inside, a corridor carved entirely of shimmering ice stretched before them, walls glittering with fractured reflections. The air that poured out was so cold it burned. Bren tested the threshold with one boot. The ice remained inert. "Stay close. If these carvings tell the truth, the vault will test us."

"Test how?" Kade asked.

"With whatever it was built to protect," Bren said grimly.

Lira tightened her grip on her pack straps, trying to steady the thundering in her chest. The Eye pulsed, tugging at her from within. Evo glanced at her, brows drawing together. "Stay right behind me. Don't let the Eye pull you too fast."

She nodded, each step sending the shard's power thrumming through her bones.

They stepped into the Frostmade Vault, into glittering walls and breath-cracking cold. Behind them, the door slid shut with a hiss.

The sound echoed like a heartbeat. Or a warning. And the vault's pale blue glow brightened, as if awakening.

CHAPTER SEVENTEEN
The Second Vault

The first chamber stretched deep into the glacier, its glittering walls curving like frozen ribs. Their footsteps echoed sharply in the icy stillness, and each breath came too thick, too fast, not from exertion, but from the creeping numbness sliding into their limbs.

"Deeper," Bren said, rubbing his arms. "The cold... it's unnatural. Meant to slow intruders."

"Slow us for what?" Evo muttered.

The answer waited at the heart of the chamber.

Another door, smaller, older, far more intricate, loomed ahead. It was carved entirely from black ice, veined with silver. No handle. No hinges. Just a puzzle of interlocking plates etched with frostbitten runes. The air here was so frigid that frost formed instantly on hair and lashes.

Kade hissed through clenched teeth. "We can't survive long in this temperature."

"That's why there's a second vault," Tamsin said, stepping forward, her eyes gleaming with challenge. "Built to stop anyone who made it past the first."

Evo rubbed his hands together. "You can open it, right?"

She smirked, rolling her chilled shoulders. "If I can't, we die. Great motivation."

Lira's fingers had gone completely numb. Even with the shards' warmth flickering faintly through her chest, the cold pressed in heavy and merciless.

Tamsin knelt before the black-ice vault, breathing gently on her fingers to keep them moving. Her tools stuck slightly to the frost as she slid them out. She paused, then slid them back.

"This door isn't about locks," she murmured. "It's about pressure points... weight shifts... timing."

She pressed a palm against one plate. It sank a breath. Another rose.

"Touch nothing," she warned without looking back.

Kade muttered, "Wasn't planning on it."

Minutes stretched, dragging. The cold deepened. Lira's knees trembled, not from fear, but from the creeping burn-to-numbness climbing her legs. Evo stumbled once, catching himself.

"Tamsin... please," he said.

"I know, Evo," she snapped, breath shaking. "I'm going as fast as, "

A click.

Then a soft grinding sound.

The black-ice plates began to rotate, sliding apart in a deadly, mesmerizing sequence. Frost gusted outward as the door split into four blossoming petals, revealing,

A hidden chamber.

Light shimmered from within the ice itself, illuminating treasures impossible and strange. Atop a pillar of carved frost rested the third shard. But it was not alone. Coins from dead kingdoms, weapons of enchanted steel, jewelry glowing faintly with dormant magic, treasures piled along the walls, some frozen into the ice, others carefully arranged.

"A dragon's ransom," Evo whispered.

"No," Bren said quietly. "A warning."

He pointed to the walls. Carved deep into the ice were runes older than those on the outer vault. They pulsed faintly as Bren read aloud, voice tight:

TOUCH NOT THE TREASURE.

THE VAULT REMEMBERS THIEVES.

A heavy silence fell, broken only by the faint hiss of frost.

Slowly, Kade stepped in front of Lira. "We take only what we came for."

Tamsin's eyes flicked across the gold, tempted, yes, but she gave a small, reluctant nod. "Not suicidal enough to ignore that."

Lira approached the pedestal, scanning the surface for any sign of where the shard had entered. Whatever wound it had made had already frozen closed, leaving no trace.

The shard pulsed with a deep, crystalline blue, the color of midnight caught in ice. It seemed to recognize her as she drew near, pulsing gently in response.

Her fingers closed around it. Warmth poured into her, immediate and complete. Not violent, not jagged like the serpent shard. This one sank into her as effortlessly as a sigh.

A soft hum thrummed through her ribs as the shard fused with the others she carried. Three became one, locking together with quiet certainty.

A vision struck her.

A sky torn by shadow.

A crown that glowed with fractured light.

Two shards still missing.

Nothing more. No locations. No warnings. Only the knowledge that five pieces existed and she now held three.

The vision dissolved as abruptly as it had come, leaving her breathless.

Kade's hand rested lightly on her shoulder. "Lira? You back?"

She nodded. "There are only two more shards. But I don't know where they are."

"The Eye will," Bren said, motioning toward her pack.

Lira drew it out. The crystal surface shimmered, flickered, and then steadied, blooming with golden light. Shapes formed within its depths, a shifting trail of mountains and valleys map revealing a single clear direction.

Kade exhaled slowly. "Well. Looks like we know where we're headed. The royal woods."

Tamsin flexed her fingers, still stiff from the cold. "Great. Let's get out of this frozen death tube."

But as they turned toward the door, the vault trembled, a single, warning shiver. It was subtle, almost imperceptible, but it carried intent, as if the chamber itself had noticed something missing.

Everyone froze.

Nothing else happened. No avalanche of ice. No frost beasts stirred. No traps snapped shut.

The chamber simply... watched them.

And because no one had dared touch the treasure, it allowed them to leave.

Tamsin was the first to exhale. "Well... that's new. A vault with self-control."

"Don't jinx it," Evo muttered.

One by one, they crossed into the first chamber. The moment the last of Bren's broad shoulders cleared the threshold, the great black-ice petals slammed shut with a thunderous crack that echoed like a glacier splitting.

They all flinched, but the doors did not reopen, nor did any new frost trap spring.

"Let's move," Kade said. "Before it changes its mind."

They hurried through the tunnels of shining ice, breath fogging so thickly it curled around them like smoke. The cold gnawed at exposed skin, but the fused shards within Lira warmed her from the inside, soft, thrumming, powerful.

She felt stronger.

Steadier.

Whole.

And that terrified her almost as much as it reassured her.

At last, they reached the mouth of the Frostmade Vault, a jagged archway of ice opening out into a white-glittering gorge.

Bren clapped his hands together. "Sunlight. Gods bless."

"Don't celebrate yet," Evo said, already scanning the ridgelines. "We're not alone."

The air shifted.

A low, hollow moan rolled across the gorge like wind dragged through a dying throat.

Lira felt her breath catch. "That sound, "

"Wraith," Kade said sharply. "Weapons!"

The shadows in the gorge folded inward, swirling into an inhuman-shaped mass of icy mist. Long limbs. A hollow chest. A face with no features, only a dark slit where a mouth should be.

An ice wraith.

Its voice scraped like breaking icicles. "Thief... of... crown... pieces..."

Kade stepped in front of Lira. "It's after her. Keep it off, "

The wraith lunged.

It moved like a storm of frost. One swirling arm knocked Bren off balance; another swept Evo aside. Tamsin ducked under a tendril of shadow-ice and slashed at the creature, but her blade passed through like light through fog.

"Lira, run!" Kade barked.

She couldn't. Her legs froze, not from fear, but because the wraith's reach enveloped her like a net of winter wind.

It wrapped around her torso and lifted her from the ground.

Her feet left the ice. "Kade!" she choked.

He didn't hesitate. He sprinted up a ridge of snow and launched himself off it, lasso already in hand. He'd ripped free a coil of climbing rope from his pack the moment the creature wrapped itself around her.

Evo, seeing his aim, shouted, "Kade, NOW!"

Kade threw the lasso.

It sailed wide, then snapped tight around the wraith's upper form, a form that had to remain solid if it wanted to hold on to its prize.

Kade yanked, muscles straining, boots skidding across ice. "Pull!"

Bren charged forward with a roar, grabbing the rope behind Kade. Evo scrambled in after, feet sliding dangerously close to the gorge's drop. Tamsin seized the tail end, heels digging into the snow.

Together, they pulled.

The wraith shrieked, an unearthly, bone-shivering sound, as it was dragged downward, Lira still clutched in its icy grip.

"Hold on, Lira!" Tamsin cried.

Lira gasped as cold sliced into her ribs like knives. She felt her warmth, her strength, her very self being pulled toward the creature.

A whisper filled her ear. "Crown... bearer... claimed..."

"No," she rasped. "Let, me, go!"

She drove her elbow into the wraith's chest, pointless, yet filled with every ounce of will she possessed. The shards inside her pulsed, a flare of heat blooming across her chest.

The wraith recoiled, just enough.

Kade roared, "BREN, DO IT!"

Bren heaved forward, swinging his massive axe in a wide, brutal arc.

The blade struck the wraith's chest.

Ice exploded.

The creature shattered into a storm of frost shards that blasted across the gorge like a broken glacier caught in a gale.

Lira dropped.

Kade caught her before she hit the ground, his arms locking around her as she collapsed against him, trembling.

"You're alright," he breathed, voice raw. "I've got you."

The others stumbled in close, panting, bruised, shaken, but alive.

Evo wiped frost from his face. "That thing... it was waiting for us."

"For her," Tamsin corrected.

Lira swallowed hard, pressing a hand to her chest where the fused shards still glowed faintly beneath her skin.

Kade's grip tightened protectively around her. "Whatever's hunting her is getting desperate."

"The wraith king," Bren grunted, lifting his axe again. "Let him get desperate. We'll keep smashing his pets."

"Thieves -two, wraiths -zero," Tamsin added.

But Evo's eyes scanned the horizon, uneasy.

"I don't think that was desperation," he murmured.

"I think that was a warning."

"Whatever it was, we'll deal with it. Now, let's get out of here and thaw in the forest," Kade said.

CHAPTER EIGHTEEN
The Dream of Stolen Light

The forest lay still around them, dark trunks rising like pillars, branches whispering in the wind above their small camp. After the long journey from the Frostmade Gorge, no one had complained when Kade declared they were stopping for the night. Even Bren had slumped against a fallen log with a grateful grunt.

Lira curled beneath her blanket, the fused shards thrumming softly inside her chest. They pulsed insistently, pointing the way forward, the next shard somewhere in these woods. She closed her eyes, letting exhaustion take her, and drifted into sleep.

But the dream did not feel like sleep.

It felt like being pulled.

Dragged.

A presence, vast and cold and hungry, coiled around her mind like smoke.

Then she saw it.

A clearing of blackened trees. A pedestal hewn from a tree trunk. A shard resting atop it, glowing faintly blue. And a hand closing around it.

A man made of shadows and bone, a shape that flickered like frost smoke, a crown of ice cracking across his skull.

The Wraith King.

He lifted the shard and whispered a single word:

"Mine."

The forest in the dream split open with a silent scream. Darkness swallowed the pedestal. The shard vanished into his grasp as if it had always belonged there.

Lira tried to shout. Tried to move. Tried to reach, but her limbs were frozen.

Then the Wraith King turned. His hollow eyes found her.

"You are already too late," he rasped, his voice breaking like winter branches. "And you will bring me the rest."

His hand reached toward her, and the dream shattered.

Lira bolted upright, her own scream fading into the night, heart pounding, shards burning hot beneath her skin.

Kade was already at her side, awake on watch. "Lira? What happened?"

Evo jerked awake next, nearly tumbling off his bedroll. Tamsin groaned, rubbing her eyes as she sat up. Bren snorted, startled, his hand reaching instinctively for his axe.

"You screamed," Kade said. "Loud."

Lira swallowed hard. "I... I saw him."

"Who?" Evo asked.

"The Wraith King."

Silence fell over the camp.

Kade leaned forward, jaw tightening. "Tell us."

She told them everything, the pedestal, the forest clearing, the shard glowing atop its resting place, and the Wraith King taking it, claiming it, speaking to her as though he had reached through her sleep with his own hand.

When she finished, only the fire crackled in reply.

Tamsin exhaled slowly. "Dreams from the shards must mean something. But that, "

"That wasn't a normal dream or shard vision," Evo said, his voice low and tight. "That one was like the Wraith King wanted you to see it, not the shard or the Eye."

Bren crossed his arms. "So what? We hurry. We get there first."

Lira shook her head. "We're already too late. He has it."

Kade studied her carefully. "Check. We need to be sure. Use the Eye."

Lira hesitated, then reached into her pack and withdrew the Eye. The moment her fingers curled around the ancient metal, the golden smoke within it stirred.

The Eye opened.

Everyone leaned closer.

The swirling gold twisted, shifted, and reformed into a single image.

It was not the forest floor where the shard had been hours before.

It was a towering stone cliff, jagged and sun-baked, rising above a breathtaking valley.

At the very top sat a nest the size of a wagon, woven from bones and tree limbs.

A griffin's nest.

And in the center of the nest, a faint blue glimmer caught the light.

Tamsin muttered under her breath, "Well, this will be fun."

"It wasn't there before," Evo said, his tone uneasy. "It moved. The dream actually happened."

Kade's expression darkened. "Meaning the Wraith King reached it before us."

"And he took it," Bren muttered. "So the Eye is showing us the next shard because he already has the one we were tracking."

Silence fell.

The shards burned faintly inside Lira, responding to the Eye's vision. They recognized the distant fragment of their own whole. Her dream felt real, too real.

The Wraith King had not just beaten them to a shard. He was guiding them. Waiting. Setting a trap.

Tamsin folded her arms tightly. "If we go after this shard, we might be walking straight into his plan."

Evo nodded grimly. "Exactly. He's letting us gather them for him."

Lira stared at the glowing image in the Eye, the towering cliff, the nest, the shard glinting like a star. Her voice was quiet, but steady. "It doesn't matter."

Kade blinked at her. "Lira, "

"We need to get the shards," she said firmly. "No matter where they are or who holds them." She clenched her hands and drew a slow, steadying breath. "We get ahead of him."

Bren's grin was sharp. "That's the spirit."

Evo still looked uneasy, but he nodded. "Then before sunrise, we head for the cliffs. No stopping."

Tamsin sighed. "I've always wanted to meet a griffin. I just hoped it wouldn't be guarding a shard on a death climb."

Lira slipped the Eye back into her pack, feeling its warmth fade.

Kade's gaze stayed on her, protective, steady, fierce. "Whatever trap he's setting," he said quietly, "we'll break it."

The night wind rustled through the trees, carrying a distant cry across the dark sky. Half screech, half thunder.

Lira shivered, not from the cold, but from the certainty settling into her bones. The race had already begun.

And the Wraith King was no longer behind them. He was waiting ahead.

CHAPTER NINETEEN
The Descent to the Nest

By midmorning, the forest had thinned, the trees giving way to scattered pockets of shade as the ground sloped upward. Heat shimmered off the rocks, and dust clung to their boots with every step. Still, the land was breathtaking in its harshness.

The Eye never wavered. Every time Lira touched it, the golden swirl pointed them toward the cliffs.

They reached them just past noon.

The cliff face rose before them like a towering wall of gray stone, jagged and sun-baked, carved by time into ridges and deep shadows. Hot, restless winds swept up its height, carrying the faint scent of feathers and something sharp, like ozone after a storm.

High on the stone, perched on a jut of rock like some ancient throne, sat the griffin's nest.

It was a massive tangle of branches, bones, and sun-bleached driftwood. A raw, wild construction that could have swallowed a horse whole. At its center, half-hidden in the woven mass, Lira caught the faint glimmer of blue light.

The shard.

Evo let out a low whistle. "Well... that's definitely a nest."

Tamsin grimaced. "And definitely high."

Bren squinted. "Is the griffin home?"

Kade scanned the sky. "Not that I can see. But they don't stay gone for long."

Lira stepped closer to the cliff's edge. The drop below was dizzying. The stone offered handholds, but none led directly to the nest. Climbing from below would mean hanging almost free in places, the nest looming above them like a trap.

Kade followed her gaze. "You're thinking the same thing I am."

"That climbing up is suicide?" Tamsin asked.

"Exactly," Kade said. "One slip of the rock, one swoop from the griffin, and we'd have nothing beneath our feet."

Evo groaned. "Please tell me the alternative is better."

"It is," Lira said quietly. "We climb down."

They all turned to look at her.

She pointed toward the cliff's crown. "If we get above the nest, the descent will be straight. The rock is more even near the top. And if something attacks, we'll have leverage from above. We'll be secured, and the others can hold the rope."

Bren folded his arms. "She's right. It's a cleaner drop from the top."

Kade nodded. "Then we go around. There's a rise to the east. It should lead us above the ledge."

They hiked for nearly twenty minutes, circling the base of the cliff until the slope rose sharply. Loose stones scraped their boots as the sun baked their necks, dry shrubs clinging stubbornly to the rock. Wind whispered through them as they pushed upward.

At the summit, the ground opened into a narrow spine of stone stretching toward the cliff's crown with a spattering of shade trees. They crossed it carefully, the valley yawning far below.

Finally, they stood directly above the griffin's nest, close enough that the woven mass of branches and bones was visible beneath the lip of the cliff.

Evo shuddered. "That is... a very big nest."

Tamsin wrapped her arms around herself. "And we're about to lower them into it. This is fine. Everything is fine."

Bren unhooked the climbing rope from his pack. "Let's set up."

Kade turned to Lira. "You ready?"

She nodded, though her stomach twisted with nerves and the pull of the shard burning faintly inside her.

They tied the rope around Lira's waist, securing the knot with practiced precision. The wind stirred across the cliff top, warm and restless. Kade tied the second rope around his own waist.

Lira blinked at him. "Kade, "

"No," he said firmly. "I'm not letting you go down there alone."

"But the griffin, "

"Doesn't change this." His voice softened but remained unshakable. "You fall, I fall. That's how this works."

Her chest tightened, not from fear, but something deeper.

"Fine," she whispered.

Evo, Bren, and Tamsin anchored themselves. Bren braced his boots against a boulder, holding Kade's rope; Evo looped his rope around a tree for leverage; Tamsin dug her heels into a stone crack. They held Lira's rope, the three of them taking up the combined weight, faces tense and ready.

"Keep watch," Kade said. "Griffins spot prey from miles off."

Tamsin muttered, "Wonderful."

Kade gave one last nod and guided Lira to the edge of the cliff.

"Ready?" he asked.

She swallowed hard, palms slick with sweat. "Ready."

Together, they swung their legs over the edge.

The rope tightened immediately. The others adjusted their hold with practiced precision. Kade descended first, Lira just above him. He guided her carefully when the footholds narrowed, every movement deliberate.

Dust rained down with each step. The stone beneath them was hot and rough, scraping their palms and sending tiny flecks of grit into the air.

The nest grew closer.

Close enough now for Lira to smell it, sun-warmed feathers mingled with the unmistakable musk that griffins carried wherever they went.

Kade braced himself, lowering even more cautiously.

"We're almost level," he murmured. "Just a little more, "

A shadow swept across the cliff.

Massive.

Fast.

The rope jerked in Tamsin's hands. She gasped.

Evo cursed under his breath.

Bren's grip tightened like iron.

Kade went utterly still.

Lira froze, fingertips digging into the stone.

Above them, a piercing screech shredded the sky.

Close. Circling back.

Kade's voice fell to a razor-edged whisper.

"Lira... move."

The screech cut through the heat-thick air, slicing down Lira's spine. The wind shifted violently, no longer a steady warm gust but a sudden, forceful blast as enormous wings beat the sky.

"Down, now!" Kade hissed.

Lira didn't think. She slid the last three feet of the cliff face, boots skidding on stone. She dropped onto the outer rim of the nest, and the branches groaned beneath her weight.

Kade landed a heartbeat later, knees bending to absorb the impact. He grabbed her arm, yanking her clear of the edge just as a shadow swallowed the sun.

The griffin dove.

The wind from its wings slammed into them like a battering force, grit stinging Lira's eyes and shoving her backward. Kade braced himself between her and the creature, sword already drawn.

Above, Tamsin's voice cracked with panic.

"It's right on top of you!"

"Hold the rope!" Bren bellowed.

The griffin struck the nest's rim with a thunderous crack. Driftwood and bone splintered under its talons, debris cascading down the cliffside.

Evo's voice rang from above, strained and shaking.

"It's circling, coming back!"

"Stay low!" Kade barked.

The griffin reared its massive head. Golden eyes blazed like wildfire. Faint threads of lightning crackled across its beak and feathers, an electric shimmer dancing over its sun-warmed plumage.

Lira's breath hitched. She had seen griffins in books, but nothing had prepared her for the sheer, terrifying reality of one up close.

The creature lunged again.

Kade shoved her aside just in time. The beak snapped shut where she had been standing a heartbeat earlier. The nest shuddered violently, branches groaning under the assault.

"Kade, we can't stay up here long!" Lira shouted, scrambling toward the center of the nest.

He didn't answer. He was too busy deflecting a swipe of razor-sharp talons. His blade sparked against the griffin's claws, the shock shooting up his arm.

Lira spotted it. Near the middle of the nest, half buried beneath a spill of feathers and brittle bones, the shard pulsed with a faint but insistent blue light, like a heartbeat wrapped in frost.

"Kade! I see it!" she called.

He risked a glance. "Get it!"

She sprinted across the unsteady woven surface. The nest dipped beneath her weight, swaying like a basket suspended over the cliff. She dropped to her knees, shoving aside debris, hands trembling as she reached for the shard.

A blast of hot air hit her back. The griffin had turned toward her.

Kade swore and lunged, driving his blade into the creature's shoulder to distract it. The griffin shrieked, wings flaring outward, huge, sunlit, and powerful enough to buffet Lira sideways.

She slid dangerously close to the rim.

"Lira!" Kade roared.

She grabbed a jut of bone, stopping her fall by sheer luck and instinct. Heart hammering, she dragged herself back toward the center and reached again.

Her fingers finally closed around the shard. Cold flooded through her palm. Not the cold of shade or winter, but a deep, ancient chill, sharp enough to sting her skin. The shard pulsed, glowing brighter the moment she touched it. The Eye at her chest flared in response, heat shimmering beneath her clothes.

"It's reacting," she whispered.

The griffin shrieked again, fury rolling off it in waves.

Kade struggled to keep its attention, dodging a flurry of wing strikes that sent dust and fragments of the nest flying. He stumbled back, nearly losing his footing.

Lira turned, clutching the shard to her chest. "I've got it!"

"Then get ready to move!" he shouted, parrying another blow.

Above, the rope jerked. Tamsin, Evo, and Bren were pulling hard, trying to give them lift.

"We're bringing you up!" Bren yelled down.

The griffin wheeled, wings beating fiercely, preparing to strike again. This time it angled directly for Lira.

She braced herself.

The shard responded first. A sudden burst of icy wind exploded outward from her grip, sharp, bright, and shockingly cold against the sweltering cliff heat. Frost leapt across the nearest branches, spreading in jagged lines.

The griffin faltered mid-lunge, startled.

Kade seized the opening. He darted forward and grabbed Lira around the waist.

"Hold tight!"

The rope snapped taut, jerking them upward off the nest just as the griffin slashed through the space where they had been.

The nest tore apart beneath its claws, branches snapping like brittle bones, shards plummeting into the canyon below.

Lira clung to Kade as they swung out from the cliff, wind roaring past them, the shard burning cold against her chest.

Above, the others strained, hauling them up hand over hand.

The griffin screamed in rage.

It lunged upward, chasing them along the jagged cliff face.

"Faster!" Evo shouted.

"We're trying!" Tamsin cried back.

The creature closed the distance. Its talons reached, and the heat of its breath scorched Lira's back.

Kade twisted, shielding her, putting himself between Lira and the griffin.
Bren braced with every muscle in his body and yelled, "Hold on!"

The rope jerked violently. Lira's stomach lurched as she and Kade shot upward like stones from a sling, out of reach, just as the griffin's talons snapped shut on empty air.

Its furious roar echoed off the cliffs while they were pulled swiftly toward the top.

They were not safe yet, but they were rising. The shard pulsed cold and bright in Lira's hand.

The cliff edge rushed toward them, too fast, too steep, their bodies swinging painfully against the sunbaked rock. Kade's shoulder slammed into the stone, and he gritted out a curse, but he never loosened his hold on Lira.

"Almost there!" Bren roared from above.

Hands reached down. Tamsin grabbed Kade's forearm. Evo caught Lira by the back of her tunic. Bren anchored the rope, muscles straining. Together, with a final heave, they hauled Kade and Lira over the lip of the cliff.

Lira collapsed onto hot stone, breathing hard, dust scratching her throat. Kade landed beside her, rolling onto one knee and lifting his sword before his feet were even under him.

Evo panted, "Is it still, "

A shadow swallowed the sun.

The griffin shot downward in a violent burst of wind, talons scraping the cliff face as it surged toward them. Its wings beat with thunderous force, sending pebbles skittering across the stone.

Tamsin screamed, "It's coming!"

Kade stepped in front of Lira. Bren raised his axe. Evo drew his daggers. Heat shimmered around them, and dust whirled through the blasts of wind.

Then the griffin lunged onto the cliff top. Its claws slammed into stone with a ground-shaking impact. Lightning crackled through its feathers. Its golden eyes locked on Lira, not Kade, not the others. Lira.

It recognized the shard as its treasure. It wanted it back.

Lira staggered to her feet, clutching the shard tightly in her palm. It pulsed wildly, blue light flickering like a nervous heartbeat. She stumbled backward as the griffin screeched, lowering its head to strike again.

"Lira! Move!" Kade yelled.

She didn't. She couldn't. Something inside her, deep in her chest where the fused shards already lived, was burning.

The shard in her hand answered the others within her. A line of cold shot up her arm, spreading into her chest like a winter storm igniting from the inside.

The griffin lunged.

Kade threw himself toward her, but he wasn't fast enough.

The world snapped.

Lira absorbed the shard.

Blue light exploded from her hand, shooting through her skin, rippling across her ribs and spine. Her breath hitched, and her head snapped back as the shard's power collided with the storm of shards already fused within her.

A shockwave of cold blasted outward.

It struck everyone, Kade, Bren, Evo, Tamsin, but only as a numbing chill.

The griffin, though, was not so fortunate.

It shrieked. Its wings recoiled, feathers crackling with frost and raw energy as the cold tore through its supercharged aura. The creature stumbled backward, claws scraping furrows into the stone. Ice laced its beak, its talons, and its eyes.

Lira's pulse thundered, and her vision blurred at the edges.

The three shards inside her surged, welcoming the fourth. They pulled it deeper, locking it into place with a silent, bone-deep snap that only she could feel.

Then the power erupted. Lira raised her hand, not entirely by her own will.

A blast of blue-white energy shot forward, shaped like wind and ice, stealing the breath from the world itself.

It struck the griffin square in the chest.

The creature let out a strangled shriek, not of pain, but of instinctive terror, and leapt backward off the cliff. Its wings snapped open, shedding frost with every stroke, struggling to regain lift.

The griffin spiraled downward.

For a terrifying moment, Lira thought she had killed it.

Then its great wings caught the air.

The beast leveled out.

With a final furious screech at the cliff's edge, it beat its wings once more and fled across the valley, shrinking into a golden shape against the bright blue sky.

The instant it was gone, the power inside her dimmed.

Lira dropped to her knees, palms pressed to the hot stone.

Silence swallowed the cliff.

Kade was the first to move. He knelt beside her, hands on her shoulders, eyes searching her face with urgent concern.

"Lira," he breathed. "Are you, are you okay?"

She tried to answer. Her voice was barely a whisper. "It's inside me now. All four."

Bren exhaled slowly, lowering his axe. "Four shards..."

Evo rubbed the back of his neck. "And she just blasted a griffin off a cliff."

Tamsin crouched close, eyes wide. "That wasn't normal power, Lira. That was... something else."

Lira swallowed hard.

She could still feel the shards, fusing, shifting, humming like a storm ready to break, all four pieces now bound to her heartbeat, waiting for the last two.

She looked toward the horizon, chest aching. "We need to move," she whispered.

Kade's hand closed around hers, not pulling, not restraining, just steadying.

"We will," he said. "Together."

The wind swept across the cliff as the dust settled, warm and restless, carrying the faint echo of a griffin's scream.

CHAPTER TWENTY
The Final Signal

The heat of the cliff still radiated through the stone long after the griffin had vanished into the sky. The group wasted no time gathering the ropes, checking their packs, and backing away from the exposed ledge. Every few steps, they glanced upward, half expecting the creature to wheel around for another strike.

But the sky remained empty.

Lira moved carefully, feeling the weight of the fourth shard humming within her ribs, a steady, unsettling pulse that made her skin prickle with cold despite the dry heat rising from the rock. Kade stayed close, brushing her elbow with his hand whenever the terrain sloped sharply underfoot.

Bren was the first to break the silence as they began their descent from the ridge.

"Well," he grunted, "that could have gone worse."

"That could have gone much worse," Tamsin corrected, wiping sweat from her brow. "Like 'buried in a griffin's nest' worse."

"Or 'dropped off a cliff' worse," Evo added.

Kade did not laugh. "We need distance. That blast you let out, Lira, will have been seen for miles."

Lira tensed. "I didn't mean to, "

"You saved all of us," he cut in firmly. "That is what matters."

She nodded, though unease sat heavy in her throat.

By the time they reached solid ground at the base of the cliffs, the sun had arced toward late afternoon, casting long shadows across the valley floor. They stopped only once, beneath the shade of a stunted tree whose dark branches twisted like broken fingers.

Tamsin sank onto a rock. "All right. Before something else with wings tries to kill us, check the Eye."

They all turned to Lira.

She hesitated, not out of fear of the Eye itself, but fear of what it might reveal. Still, she reached into her pack and drew it out.

The metal warmed instantly to her touch, the golden smoke inside stirring awake. The others leaned in, dust and heat clinging to their clothes, their breaths held tight.

Lira exhaled slowly. "Show us the next shard."

The Eye opened.

Gold swirled.

It shifted.

It formed into an image.

A ruined plain.

Black stone.

A fortress twisted by shadow.

A throne of obsidian and bone.

And on the throne sat a man of frost, smoke, and death.

The Wraith King.

In his hand pulsed a faint blue light, the fifth shard.

Lira's stomach hollowed.

Evo whispered, "So he still has it... just checking."

Tamsin's voice cracked. "And he is not hiding it. He wants us to see. He wants us to come."

Bren spat into the dust. "It's a trap. Obviously."

Kade remained silent, his jaw tight, eyes locked on the shard clutched in the Wraith King's hand. Then he spoke, low and steady: "Trap or not, we have to go. We need that shard."

Evo ran a hand through his hair. "Yeah, but he's stronger than before. Every time we've seen him, he's closer. More solid." His voice dropped. "And now he has a shard of his own."

Lira swallowed, feeling the four inside her pulse like answering drums. "He wants all of them," she said quietly. "That's why he's letting us find them. That's why he isn't attacking anymore."

Bren frowned. "So what? He wanted you to collect them for him?"

"Yes," Kade said sharply. "The shards are in her now. If he gets Lira, "

"He gets everything," Tamsin finished, pale.

Silence settled thick around them.

Lira closed the Eye, but its weight did not leave her hand. Her breath felt thin, her chest tight under the pressure of four shards whispering like distant storms.

Finally, she said, "We need a plan."

Kade nodded. "We can't march straight into his stronghold without one."

"Then let's think," Evo said, sitting cross-legged. "We know he has one shard. Lira has four. He needs her, but he does not want to kill her, or he would have tried harder."

"He wants her alive," Tamsin agreed. "Which means, "

"She's leverage," Bren finished. "Or the key."

Lira looked at them all, voice steady even though her fingers shook. "He wants me to come to him. So we use that."

Kade's eyes flashed. "Not as bait."

"Not bait," she said softly. "Leverage of our own. He thinks we will walk into his trap unprepared or overconfident."

Evo raised a brow. "Or both... but we won't."

"No," Lira said. "This time we will walk in knowing exactly what he wants. And we will know how to fight so he does not get it."

Bren cracked his knuckles. "So the plan is: out-think, out-run, and out-fight a death king made of smoke and frost." He shrugged. "Easy."

Tamsin groaned. "I'm going to pretend he didn't say that."

Kade stepped closer to Lira, his voice low enough that only she, and the shards, could hear. "We will protect you. Whatever we walk into, we do it together. And we will get that last shard."

Lira nodded, but her gaze drifted toward the direction the Eye had shown. Toward the ruins. Toward the throne. Toward the Wraith King. And toward the final piece of the power humming inside her bones.

She breathed in once, steadying herself. "Then we move," she whispered. "Before he decides to come to us instead."

The group gathered their packs. They turned toward the distant black horizon. The final leg of the journey began.

CHAPTER TWENTY-ONE
The Forging Before the Final Night

Dawn never truly reached the ravine. What little light filtered down the cliffs slid along the stone in thin, metallic streaks, leaving the world steeped in a pallid gray. The air felt heavy, as though the sun itself hesitated to look too closely at what lingered below.

Lira kept one hand pressed to her ribs and the other wrapped tightly around the Eye. Beneath her palm, the four fused shards throbbed in steady rhythm, like a second heart beating out of time with her own. Each pulse was a reminder of what she carried and what hunted her for it.

Evo was the first to break the silence, his voice rough from too many sleepless nights.

"Show us," he said. "Where's the last one?"

Lira lifted the Eye. Dark currents swirled beneath its glassy surface, clouds trapped in miniature, then slowly thinned and parted. The image sharpened until it revealed a throne room of nightmares.

The Wraith King sat upon a towering throne that seemed shaped from ancient bone turned to obsidian. In his fist, the fifth shard pulsed with black light, trembling as if straining to escape his grasp. Around him drifted wraiths formed of smoke and screaming faces, phasing in and out of existence as though reality itself refused to anchor them.

Lira's breath caught in her throat.

"Nothing's changed," she murmured. "He knows we're coming."

"He wants us to," Kade replied, tightening his grip on his sword. "He's waiting for us to bring the crown together for him."

"Which means we walk straight into his trap," Tamsin said quietly, her fingers brushing the hilts at her sides.

Bren exhaled, his shoulders tense. "But we can't leave that shard with him. If we don't put the crown back together, the prophecy will unfold exactly as it was written. And the crown must choose a new ruler."

"He will rip the others out of me," Lira added, her voice barely above a whisper. "And the realm will die with me."

The silence that followed settled over them like frost.

Evo stepped closer, jaw set with resolve. "Then we prepare. We take weapons forged for this war, and we take that shard before he takes everything from us. We go to the Forger."

They reached the hidden forge by midday. It revealed itself as a narrow fissure in the mountainside, glowing faintly, pulsing like a living vein of light. Heat rolled from within the cavern, but it was not ordinary flame that illuminated the depths.

It was power.

The Weapon's Forger was a solitary immortal born of Nephilim blood, neither wholly divine nor wholly mortal. He had been shaped by an ancient purpose: to craft weapons capable of turning the fate of kingdoms, but only for those whose hearts remained uncorrupted. Legends claimed his forge burned with celestial fire, a flame that recognized truth as readily as it scorched falsehood. Any who approached him with deceit invited annihilation. Those who came with honor might earn a weapon alive with enchantment, bound to its bearer and loyal only to a worthy cause.

Though ageless, he rarely intervened in mortal affairs. He waited for champions forged by choice rather than lineage, souls willing to shoulder the burden of shaping the realms' future.

Master Ralven stood waiting as they entered, as though he had counted the very steps that brought them to his threshold. His skin bore a tapestry of old burn scars, and his eyes gleamed like steel hammered flat upon an anvil.

"I know why you have come," he said. "The Eye sent me a most interesting dream."

Behind him, weapons hung suspended in the heated air. Half-formed blades shimmered in shifting silhouettes, spears flickered between shape and smoke, and raw energy crackled like lightning caught in glass.

Ralven motioned them forward one by one. He placed a scarred hand over each of their chests, feeling something deeper than a heartbeat.

He began with Kade.

From the molten air, he drew forth a sword that shimmered as though struggling to remain in the mortal world. Its edges glinted with a spectral sheen designed to force a wraith into solidity.

Next came Bren.

Ralven shaped a massive battle-axe, heavy as judgment itself. Its haft was wrapped in obsidian leather, and its broad blade bore runes that glowed in slow, steady pulses.

For Evo, he split the heated metal into two perfect halves, forging twin daggers whose edges hummed with the faint echo of trapped voices.

"Speed is your strength," the Forger said. "Strike swiftly, and give the wraiths no time to fade."

For Tamsin, he crafted twin sai in mirrored symmetry, their prongs honed keen enough to tear through incorporeal shadow.

"These will anchor what has forgotten its shape," Ralven told her. "Pin them to reality."

At last, he stood before Lira.

He did not immediately turn to the forge. Instead, he studied her as the four fused shards glowed faintly beneath her skin, tracing pulsing patterns of light across her ribs.

"What she requires," he murmured, "has never existed."

He reached into the furnace with his bare hands.

The mountain trembled in response.

When he withdrew them, a form hovered between his palms, neither blade nor staff nor any familiar instrument of war. It was a conduit wrought of spiraled metal and crystal, designed to amplify the shards' power and channel it like a storm bound within glass.

"For you," Ralven said softly. "A weapon born for the shards themselves. It will answer to no one else."

The forge flared brighter, its radiance washing the cavern walls in gold and white.

"There is more," Ralven continued. He turned once more to the flame and drew out five sets of armor etched with angelic runes. The plates were thin, almost delicate in appearance, and light shimmered along their surfaces like breath upon glass.

They accepted the armor with gratitude, though they doubted its strength. When they donned it, the metal shifted and settled, molding itself perfectly to each wearer as though it had always known their shape.

Outside, danger pressed closer.

Evo moved to the entrance, narrowing his eyes toward the distant horizon. "They are still there. The palace hunters."

"They have not attacked," Bren said, unease creeping into his voice.

"Because they are waiting," Tamsin answered. "Waiting for us to finish what they cannot. Waiting until the crown is whole."

"And then they will strike," Kade said.

Lira tightened her grip on the conduit. The shards within her answered with a steady, rising hum.

"Then we will be ready."

The forge lights flared one final time, shadows twisting along the cavern walls like living things.

The final war was coming, and their enemies, both living and dead, were closing in.

At last the forge dimmed, its molten brilliance receding until only embers cast flickering light across the stone. Lira stood at the chamber's center, holding the conduit with both hands. It vibrated faintly, almost breathing, attuned to the four shards humming within her chest.

Ralven circled her once, nodding with grim reverence. "It is attuned more perfectly than I dared hope. The shards recognize what was made for them."

Warmth flowed from the conduit into her palms, up her arms, and into her ribs. The resonance felt steady and sure.

It did not feel like a weapon.

It felt like a promise.

Kade stepped beside her. "Does it hurt?"

"No," Lira said softly. "It feels like it has always belonged to me."

Ralven offered them a final warning before they departed.

"Fight clean. Fight as one. Remember that wraiths fear only what they cannot consume."

With that, they left the mountain forge behind and began the long march toward the Wraith King's fortress, a black citadel rising in the distance like a broken tooth thrust from the world itself.

CHAPTER TWENTY-TWO
The March Toward Doom

The land changed as they traveled.

The wind thinned until each breath felt stolen. The sky dulled to a flat, colorless gray. Even the light seemed stretched and strained, drawn toward the distant fortress as though it longed to be consumed.

They walked in silence for hours. With every mile, their steps grew heavier, as if the earth itself resisted them. At last, Bren broke the quiet.

"So, say we win," he said, rubbing his thumb over the runes etched into the handle of his axe. "Say we take the last shard from the Wraith King. How exactly are we supposed to get the shards out of Lira and reform the crown?"

Tamsin slowed. Evo stopped entirely. Kade froze mid-step.

Lira felt their attention shift to her like a physical weight pressing against her ribs.

"Well?" Bren asked quietly. "How do we do it without killing her?"

No one answered.

Because no one could.

Lira swallowed. Her hand drifted to her sternum, where the shards pulsed faintly beneath her skin, warm and restless. "I don't know," she whispered. "I thought the Eye would tell us. Or someone would. Or something."

Evo dragged a hand down his face. "We're about to face the Wraith King, and we don't even know if we can repair the crown afterward."

"And we can't just cut them out," Bren muttered. "We're not butchers."

Silence settled over them like snow.

Then the Eye flared to life in Lira's hand.

Heat pulsed through her fingers. She gasped as it rose from her palm, hovering weightless in the air. A beam of shimmering white light poured down onto the dead grass. The glow widened, shifted, and reshaped itself into a vision.

An ancient ruin appeared before them, half-collapsed and strangled by twisted ivy. Stone arches stood cracked but defiant, carved with symbols older than kingdoms. Broken pillars circled a vast mosaic of crowns set into the ground. At the center stood a pedestal shaped like an open hand, and upon it rested a book formed from slabs of stone.

"The Temple of the First Crown," Tamsin breathed. "I've heard of it in stories. In myths."

The vision sharpened. An inscription etched along the pedestal came into focus.

The shattered re-formed, the broken restored, the wounded healed. Only in this holy place can all three be true.

Kade stared at the image, his jaw tight. "So once we have the last shard, that is where we go."

Evo nodded slowly. "Which means the crown cannot be reformed anywhere else. I assumed the Priestess of the Royal Peaks would do it. She restores the crown when it fractures naturally."

"Perhaps it is different because it didn't break naturally," Tamsin said thoughtfully. "Perhaps it is because the queen shattered it herself."

Bren exhaled. "So the plan is to defeat the Wraith King, claim the shard, reach a ruined temple, and somehow decipher ancient stone tablets."

Lira released a shaky breath. "That is the plan."

The Eye dimmed. The vision dissolved like smoke over water, leaving only the bleak landscape around them.

Kade stepped closer to her. His posture was steady, even if fear flickered in his eyes.

"We will get you there," he said firmly. "All of us. You are not facing this alone."

One by one, the others nodded. Determination settled over them, fitting into place like armor.

The path toward the fortress darkened with every step.

But at least now they knew where they must go afterward.

And what must be done.

"Then let's go," Lira said softly.

Together, they walked deeper into the shadow of the final war.

As they continued, the air changed first.

Not the scent or the temperature. Those had shifted miles ago. It was the weight of it. The atmosphere grew thick and oppressive, as though something vast leaned closer the farther they advanced.

By the time they crossed the jagged ridge that marked the edge of the Wraith King's domain, the world had fallen silent.

No birds called. No wind stirred. No leaves rustled.

Only the muted crunch of their boots over ash-coated ground.

The land was twisted and drained of color. Gray roots coiled across lifeless soil. Towering spires of stone jutted from the earth like broken teeth. Wisps of mist curled around their legs despite the air being dry as old parchment.

Inside Lira's chest, the shards began to pulse faster. They reacted to the suffocating power that cloaked the land like a second sky.

Shapes shifted in the distance.

Bren saw them first. "Left ridge."

"On the right as well," Tamsin whispered.

Dozens of wraiths gathered among the rocks and shadows. Their forms were half-shaped, edges flickering like fading embers. Hollow eyes burned pale green as they tracked the group's every movement.

Other creatures lingered among them. Wolves black as scorched bone prowled with smoke trailing from their jaws. Tall, crooked figures stood draped in rotted armor. Yet none advanced. They simply watched.

Evo tightened his grip on his twin daggers. "Why are they not attacking?"

Kade rested his hand on his sword hilt. "Because they were commanded not to."

Lira shivered. "He wants us to reach him."

"To finish this," Bren said darkly.

They continued forward. The wraiths parted before them as though pushed aside by an unseen tide. Each step felt like a descent into a grave prepared long ago for something far older than themselves.

"What do you know about the Wraith King?" Lira asked Kade quietly.

Kade drew a steady breath. "Long before the Five Kingdoms existed, when the realm was still fractured, King Veredon the Unyielding ruled a vast nation. He was a conqueror without equal, feared for his brilliance in war and his refusal to surrender, even against impossible odds. But as the years passed and his enemies fell, Veredon became consumed by one fear. He would not allow time or death to claim what no rival ever could."

He paused before continuing.

"Whispers reached him of a forgotten deity of shadows. It was said to grant impossible power to those willing to pay its price. Desperate to outlast all threats and secure an eternal dynasty, Veredon sought the entity in the ruins of a fortress buried beneath centuries of war. Beneath that battlefield, he made his bargain. The deity promised him immortality, unending strength, and an eternal throne."

"But that would mean he should still be ruling," Lira said.

"That was his belief," Kade replied. "But the promise was a deception. When the ritual was complete, his body unraveled. The deity granted him eternity but stripped away everything mortal within him. His flesh dissolved like smoke. His heart stilled. His crown slipped from fingers that no longer existed. What remained was a hollow spirit bound not to life, but to undeath."

"The deity's final whisper echoed through him," Evo added quietly. "You wished to outlast all things, and so you shall. You will rule here and nowhere else, for all eternity."

Kade nodded. "Now Veredon reigns over the battlefield where his kingdom fell. The ruined fortress is both his throne and his prison. Twisted by rage and denied the empire he sought to preserve, he became a creature of mist and malice. A king without a crown. A monarch without a kingdom. Doomed to linger between this world and the void."

"Wow", was all that Lira could manage.

The fortress rose ahead of them, erupting from the cracked earth like a mountain carved from shadow. Its walls were jagged and uneven, as though grown rather than built. Spectral energy drifted from its battlements in slow, dying spirals.

The massive gates stood open.

No guards waited. No resistance rose.

Only an invitation.

Kade's jaw tightened. "Stay alert. He wants us to walk inside."

"And we are going to anyway," Tamsin said quietly.

"Because we must," Lira replied. "The last shard is here. With him."

They crossed the threshold.

The silence within was suffocating. Every sound echoed, boots against stone, the faint clink of weapons, the relentless pounding of Lira's heart.

Corridor after corridor lay empty. Green flames burned in iron torches along the walls, casting a sickly glow over cracked stone. A low vibration hummed through the air, growing stronger with each chamber they passed.

At last, massive double doors loomed at the end of the hall.

The throne room.

They exchanged a single look.

Then they pushed the doors open.

The chamber stretched vast and cavernous before them. Pillars rose into blackened arches. The floor was webbed with fractures that pulsed faintly with ghostly light.

And at the far end, seated upon a jagged throne carved from bone and shadow, waited the Wraith King.

CHAPTER TWENTY-THREE
The Palace of the Wraith King

He sat perfectly still upon the throne, gaunt and impossibly tall, his robes drifting around him like coils of living smoke. Above his head, his crown hung in fractured suspension, four jagged pieces hovering like broken stars caught in an unseen orbit. The shard they sought burned where his heart should have been, cold and brilliant, its light piercing through the hollow cage of his chest.

His voice slid through the chamber, soft and silken, yet edged with ice.

"Welcome, shard bearer."

Lira stiffened.

His empty gaze settled upon her breast, where the answering shards pulsed beneath her skin.

"You have brought what is mine," he said, almost pleasantly.

Kade moved without hesitation, stepping in front of her with his sword already drawn. Steel flashed in the dim light.

"No," he replied. "We came to take what's ours."

The Wraith King smiled.

The chamber shifted.

Shadows peeled themselves from the pillars. Darkness thickened in the corners. Shapes seeped from cracks in the stone like ink bleeding through parchment. In a single breath, the throne room filled with wraiths. Dozens became scores. Scores became a legion. They surrounded the company, sealing the exits in a tightening ring of smoke and malice.

Evo swore under his breath. "Ambush."

Tamsin spun, twin sai sliding into her hands with a metallic whisper. "Weapons ready."

Bren planted his boots and raised his ax, shoulders squaring. "Let them try."

The Wraith King lifted one skeletal finger.

His army charged.

A wraith lunged at Kade, its form unraveling into claws and fangs. Kade met it head on. His blade cut cleanly through its torso, and the creature burst apart into a cloud of black vapor.

Kade blinked in surprise. "Oh. That works."

Bren roared with laughter as his ax cleaved another wraith from crown to waist. The two halves split and dissolved before they struck the ground. "Ralven wasn't exaggerating."

Two more descended on Evo. He ducked beneath a slashing limb, pivoted, and drove both daggers upward. One pierced a shadowed chest, the other found the suggestion of a throat. The wraiths disintegrated at once, leaving only a curl of fading smoke.

Tamsin moved like a streak of lightning. Her sai flashed silver as she parried one attacker and thrust the other weapon through the skull of another. The wraith shrieked and vanished. She grinned, teeth bared. "I like these."

Lira didn't attack.

She couldn't, not yet.

She remained at the center, the conduit glowing in her hands. Its pulse aligned with the frantic rhythm of the shards within her chest, each beat vibrating through her bones. Wraiths surged toward her, but none reached her. Her friends cut them down before they could close the final step.

Smoke thickened around their feet, unraveling in hissing coils as each enemy fell.

Through it all, the Wraith King watched.

Then, slowly, he rose.

The air compressed as though the room itself were drawing a breath and holding it. His height seemed to stretch higher, his shadow deepening across the shattered stone.

He lifted both hands, thin and skeletal, wrapped in flickering darkness.

"Rise," he whispered.

The chamber answered.

Wraiths erupted from every surface. They poured from pillars and ceiling vaults, seeped from fissures in the floor, and tore themselves free from the walls. Hundreds answered his call. They formed a tidal wave of shrieking, smoke bodied horrors that flooded toward the companions in an unbroken surge. The air turned glacial. Torches guttered and died. The ground trembled beneath the force of their numbers.

Kade retreated toward Lira, his blade trailing wisps of evaporating shadow. "There are too many."

Bren swung his ax in a brutal arc, shattering three wraiths at once. Five more surged forward to fill the space they left behind.

Evo rolled beneath a clawed strike and buried both daggers into another phantom's throat. "This is ridiculous. There are too many."

Tamsin drove her sai through a wraith's ribs and ripped it free as the creature dissolved. "We are going to get buried alive."

Lira's gaze swept the chamber. Her companions were being driven back, swallowed inch by inch by the advancing tide. The shards within her chest pulsed wildly, their rhythm frantic and desperate.

Use it.

The queen's familiar voice rang clear within her mind.

The conduit hummed, its light intensifying in her grasp.

Now, before they fall.

"Everyone down!" Lira screamed.

Kade reacted instantly. He forced Bren and Evo to their knees. Tamsin threw herself flat against the stone without hesitation.

The wraiths rushed forward, claws outstretched.

Lira raised the conduit high above her head.

Light erupted.

A blinding beam of molten gold exploded outward from her in a sweeping arc. It scoured the chamber with radiant force, striking the foremost wraiths and obliterating them as sunlight devours mist. Shadow after shadow burst apart under the brilliance, torn into nothingness by the burning tide of her power.

The beam expanded, widening and intensifying until the throne room blazed with searing radiance.

Every wraith it touched burst apart, evaporating into drifting sparks that hissed against the stone.

The tidal wave of shadows faltered. It trembled, fractured, and then collapsed in on itself. Within seconds, it vanished entirely, leaving scorched stone and a haze of glowing dust suspended in the air like dying stars.

Only the Wraith King remained.

He lifted one skeletal hand with deliberate calm.

Everything stopped.

"Enough," he said, his voice echoing through the chamber like ice splitting across a frozen sea. "Your strength has grown beyond expectation, child."

Lira lowered the conduit, her chest heaving as the light around it dimmed. Sweat traced a burning path down her temple.

Kade rose beside her, sword steady despite the tremor in his arm. "Then surrender the shard."

The Wraith King released a soft, withered laugh that scraped against the walls.

"You believe I would yield simply because you have survived my lesser spawn?" His skull tilted slightly. "No. But perhaps you crave fairness."

Bren gave a humorless bark of laughter. "Nothing about you is fair."

The Wraith King ignored him. He spread his arms wide.

Four circles of shadow opened around him, yawning like wells of black flame. The air within them churned, thick and suffocating. From each portal rose something far more solid and far more monstrous than the lesser wraiths that had fallen.

These were older.

Heavier.

Hungrier.

Their presence alone pressed against the lungs like a weight of iron.

The first to emerge was the Molten Behemoth. It towered like a walking fortress, black iron plates fused over a body of boiling magma. Rivers of molten light pulsed through the cracks in its armor like living veins. Every breath exhaled ash and embers. Its fists were boulders wrapped in fire.

The second was the Winged Reaper. Its skeletal frame gleamed like obsidian, vast wings stretching nearly wall to wall. Talons curved from its fingers, each one as long as a sword. Where a face should have been, a screaming mask of shadow writhed without sound.

The third rose slowly, unfolding to its full and terrible height. The Six-Armed Torturer stood as tall as a siege tower. From its gaunt torso sprouted six serpentlike arms that twisted and coiled with unsettling independence. Each limb ended in hooked talons that dripped spectral venom onto the stone, where it sizzled and smoked.

The last stepped forward without sound. The Horned Shadow Assassin moved with a fluid grace that made the eye strain to follow it. Its form shifted between smoke and bone, half humanoid and half demon. Horns curved from its brow like crescent blades, and its movements left faint afterimages hanging in the air.

They formed a ring around their king.

The Wraith King extended his arms in a macabre flourish. "My children. My first devoured souls. My generals. My nightmares given flesh."

His empty eye sockets flared with ghostly fire.

"And you bring your own champions."

Kade lifted his sword, its edge catching the fading light.

Evo drew a slow breath and steadied himself, gathering power beneath his skin.

Bren rolled his shoulders and cracked his neck, fury hardening his expression.

Tamsin twirled a sai between her fingers, though the tremor in her hand betrayed her nerves.

Lira stood behind them, her heart hammering so fiercely she could feel it in her throat.

The Wraith King tapped his claws against the arm of his throne. "If your protectors defeat mine, I will relinquish the shard in my heart."

Evo's voice was low and sharp. "He never keeps his word."

Kade did not look away from the towering monsters. "We don't need his honesty. We only need his defeat."

The Wraith King raised one skeletal hand.

"Begin."

Battle One: Kade vs. the Molten Behemoth

The Molten Behemoth roared, the sound rolling through the throne room like a volcanic eruption. Stone trembled. Dust fell from the ceiling in thin streams.

It charged.

Kade sprinted forward to meet it, boots pounding hard on the scorched floor.

Their first collision shook the entire hall. Kade's blade slammed against iron and magma, ringing like a struck anvil. A burst of sparks erupted between them.

The Behemoth swung one massive fist in a brutal arc. Kade raised his sword to block. The impact drove him backward, boots carving trenches across the floor as heat blasted against his armor.

The creature charged again.

Kade ducked beneath its sweeping arm, rolled across the floor, and came up along its flank. He carved a glowing arc along its rib plates. Molten light spilled from the wound.

For an instant, victory flickered in his chest.

Then the iron plates shifted. The magma beneath surged. The wound sealed as if it had never existed.

Kade cursed under his breath.

The Behemoth turned with terrifying speed and drove a flaming fist straight into his chest. The blow lifted him from the ground and hurled him across the chamber.

He crashed into a pillar with enough force to crack the stone. Pain detonated through his ribs, though his armor absorbed the worst of the impact.

"Kade!" Lira cried. For a moment, he knelt there, breath ragged.

Then he pushed himself upright.

He wiped the blood away from his mouth with the back of his hand and lifted his sword once more.

"Not finished."

The behemoth hammered the ground, and shockwaves ripped outward. Kade leapt aside, sprinted up a fallen beam, and vaulted over its massive head. He plunged his blade down, but the creature snatched him out of the air.

Its molten fingers burned through his armor, crushing his ribs. Kade screamed.

"Kade!" Bren stepped forward, but the Wraith King's commands froze the other demons in place. They blocked anyone from interfering.

"You cannot save him," the Wraith King crooned. "This is fairness."

Kade's vision blurred. The heat scorched his skin. He rammed his sword into the behemoth's eye. The giant howled and dropped him.

Kade rolled to his feet, panting. With one last burst of strength, he drove his blade into the glowing seam across the creature's chest. The behemoth cracked, split, and exploded into a wave of molten ash. The group exhaled in relief.

But the ash swirled. It re-formed. The behemoth stood again, whole, stronger, glowing brighter.

Kade swore softly. "Oh, come on."

The Wraith King's grin widened. "My champion learns. He adapts. Each strike you land, he grows wiser."

The behemoth charged. Kade's eyes sharpened. "Then I stop fighting like a swordsman."

He fought like a survivor. He lured the beast toward a broken pillar, ducking at the last second. The creature slammed into the stone, cracking the pillar, which collapsed and buried the behemoth beneath rubble. Kade leapt, seized the exposed molten spine, and drove his sword down with a roar.

The beast shrieked and dissolved into embers. This time, it was final. Kade collapsed to one knee. Bren clasped his shoulder. "Still a show-off. Just a more exhausted one."

BATTLE TWO: BREN VS. THE WINGED REAPER

The reaper rose silently, its wings spreading like a storm cloud. Bren yanked his ax free.

"You have aerial advantage?" he spat. "I'll bring you down."

The reaper vanished into a blur. Wind shrieked as talons slashed toward Bren's throat. He barely blocked, the force throwing him backward.

The second pass came faster. Claws raked across his enchanted armor. The third strike nearly lifted him off the ground.

Bren roared and planted his ax firmly. "Come on then! Hit me again!"

The reaper screeched and dove downward. Bren spun, swinging his ax in an upward arc, cleaving its wing clean off. The creature crashed. Bren charged, burying the ax in its chest. The reaper dissolved into smoke, only to reform behind him, wing restored and talons sharper than before.

"Oh, hell," Bren muttered.

It dove again. Bren met it head-on. The battle went airborne, Bren hanging from one wing, slamming his ax repeatedly into rib and bone. They crashed in a whirlwind of feathers and shadows.

Bren rose, lungs burning. "Stay dead, damn it!" He grabbed a broken pillar chain, looped it around the creature's neck, and heaved with all his strength. The reaper shrieked as the chain tightened. Bren swung it into the nearest wall, dazing the creature, then crushed its skull with two brutal ax strikes. This time it stayed dead.

He spat blood. "Next one better not fly."

BATTLE THREE: EVO VS. THE SIX-ARMED TORTURER

The giant approached, six talons scraping stone. Evo sighed. "Of course I get the creepy one."

The creature lunged. Evo dodged six simultaneous strikes in a blur of motion, flipping over one arm, sliding between another, cutting where he could. But the wounds healed instantly. It punched him across the room. Evo slammed into a broken wall. The armor absorbed some of the impact, but not all. He coughed blood. "I hate bullies."

The giant attacked again. Evo vanished into the shadows, then reappeared behind it, slashing all six arms in a spiraling strike. The creature roared. Its arms reformed even longer.

"Oh, great," Evo muttered. "It upgrades."

The next strike pierced its shoulder. It cried out, spinning away with a dagger buried deep in bone. The giant seized Evo by the legs and slammed him into the ground.

"EVO!" Tamsin screamed.

He twisted free at the last second, rolling away as blood poured from his nose. Then he grinned, feral. "Okay. My turn."

He sprinted up the creature's back, dodging all six arms, and drove both daggers into its eye sockets. The monster convulsed, then fell. Dust swirled, and it rose again, blind but faster.

Evo barely dodged the next blow. "Fine! No eyes? Let's take your head!" He leapt, grabbed one horn-like ridge, and severed the spine at the base of its skull with both blades. The giant collapsed permanently, dissolving into smoke with a long, shrieking wail. Evo wiped blood from his lip. "Creepy. And rude."

BATTLE FOUR: TAMSIN VS. THE SHADOW ASSASSIN

The assassin stepped forward, silent, deadly, unhurried. Its eyes locked on Tamsin.

"Figures," she muttered. "The fast one wants me."

It blurred. Tamsin barely blocked the first strike. The second hit her ribs, cracking something. She rolled with the blow and sprang up, only to find the demon already behind her.

"You cannot outrun him," the Wraith King called. "He was a killer in life and a perfect one in death."

Tamsin's jaw tightened. She met the next slash, sparks flying as her sai intercepted the horned strike. She struck its shoulder, but the wound sealed instantly.

"Oh yeah... adaptation," she hissed. "Almost forgot."

The assassin launched a flurry that shredded the floor and walls. Tamsin flipped, twisted, and dodged by inches, bleeding from a dozen cuts. The creature lunged again.

She ducked under the sweeping horn and drove both sai deep into its ribs. Smoke erupted from its body, and then the demon seized her throat. Tamsin wheezed as it lifted her off the ground.

"KILL," it hissed.

Her vision dimmed. Then she twisted her wrist and dragged the sai upward, slicing through throat and skull. The assassin froze, then crumbled into ash.

Tamsin hit the ground on her knees, gasping. "Try killing me slower next time."

Silence fell. All four demon wraiths, his favored, his ancient champions, lay gone. Defeated. Destroyed. By lowly thieves wielding unexpectedly enchanted weapons.

The Wraith King rose slowly. Shadows around him coiled like a storm.

"Impossible," he whispered. "Four mortals defeating my elite?"

He stepped forward, each movement bending the light around him.

"You never fought the guild of thieves, have you?" Kade remarked.

Lira lifted her chin. "We won your trials. You made a bargain."

He leaned close. "And now," he hissed, "I choose the final trial. One reserved for those foolish enough to hope."

Silence filled the throne room. Fury rolled off him like a living tide.

Lira stepped forward before any of the others could react. Her conduit, woven gold and humming softly along her forearm, glimmered brighter at her movement, sensing the sharp rise of shard power pulsing within her.

"What is the final trial?" she asked, her voice steady despite the exhaustion wracking her limbs.

The Wraith King tilted his head, as if tasting her resolve.

"A duel," he said. "Your light against my dark. Winner takes all."

Kade hissed a curse and stepped in front of her, sword raised.

"No. If you want a fight, you go through me."

The Wraith King's laughter was low and jagged.

"You misunderstand, mortal. You think there is a choice."

Tamsin moved to Lira's side. "You don't have to do this alone."

Lira shook her head. "He'll never surrender the shard unless I face him. If I don't, we lose everything."

The Wraith King lifted his other hand, and darkness surged like a storm. Shadows spiraled around his arm, condensing into a growing vortex of malignant energy. Veins of night crawled across his skeletal frame. He was preparing something enormous. Something meant only for her.

Lira breathed deeply. Her conduit warmed against her skin. The four shards embedded within her flared, pulsing like a heartbeat.

Golden light rippled from her palms. At first a soft glow, then a brighter pulse, then a radiant flare that swallowed the shadows around her feet.

The Wraith King spread his arms.

"Come, little one. Let us see whether dawn can outshine death."

He unleashed the dark.

The blast roared toward her, a cascade of black fire and writhing tendrils, scorching void energy gouging the stone. The throne room shook with the force of it.

Lira lifted both hands and answered. Her golden shard-light, magnified by the conduit, erupted in a beam that collided with the Wraith King's power. The air buckled under the impact. Stones tore from the walls, columns trembled, and the others were thrown to their knees.

Light and darkness clashed in the center of the throne room, two storms locked in violent collision, each refusing to yield.

"LIRA!" Kade shouted over the roar, shielding his eyes.

She did not turn. She did not blink. She did not falter.

Her feet slid against the cracking stone as the Wraith King intensified his assault, forcing her backward inch by inch. Darkness spun around him like a hurricane, and his skeletal jaw twisted into a snarl.

"You are nothing," he thundered. "A child pretending at godhood."

Lira gritted her teeth. She thought of the climb through the cliffs, the griffin and the serpent, the pain of the shards fusing, her friends at her back, Kade's hand reaching for her whenever she fell.

"I'm not pretending," she whispered.

Golden brilliance erupted from her conduit, surging thicker, brighter, fiercer than ever before. Four shards burned as one, spilling through her veins like pure sunlight made alive.

The golden beam doubled in intensity. The Wraith King staggered back. His darkness cracked. Light speared forward, sharp and blinding. His roar shook the world.

The throne room detonated with power. Light and darkness poured across the stone floor in rivers of molten gold and smoking shadow. Columns split, ceilings cracked, and the Wraith King's blackened banners tore from their hooks, whipping violently through the storm.

Kade, Bren, Evo, and Tamsin fought to remain upright, sliding across the floor as the titanic forces raged between Lira and the Wraith King, two storms trying to unmake each other.

The Wraith King towered, his skeletal frame swelling with shadows bleeding from walls, ceiling, and floor. Tendrils lashed out, ripping through stone and clawing at Lira's beam of light.

"You cannot stop the night!" he roared, shaking the mountain with his voice. "This realm is my dominion, my death, my crown!"

Lira's feet dug into the fractured floor. Her conduit blazed hotter, brighter, almost too bright to look at. Her entire body glowed, her hair whipped around her in arcs of white-gold, and her skin shimmered with veins of molten shard-light.

"I'm not here to take your crown," she shouted, her voice breaking with power. "I'm here to take mine."

The Wraith King bellowed, thrusting both hands forward. Darkness surged like a tidal wave, crashing into her and slamming her backward.

Stone exploded as she skidded across the floor, barely bracing before the shadows could consume her.

"LIRA!" Kade yelled.

The Wraith King lunged, faster than a corpse should move, faster than shadow should flow. His claws descended toward her heart. She twisted, thrusting the conduit upward.

Golden fire erupted. The blast tore the Wraith King from his feet and hurled him into a pillar, shattering it into dust. The surrounding wraiths shrieked and dissolved into ash from the shockwave.

He rose again, enraged.

He slammed his hands together, and the entire throne room split open. A vortex of swirling shadow exploded outward, tearing up the floor, swallowing the banners, and dragging debris into a spiraling storm.

"Fall!" he thundered.

Lira stood tall, gold blazing behind her like wings.

"Never."

She slammed her palms together. The four shards inside her erupted in perfect unity. A halo of pure golden energy encircled her, then blasted outward in a colossal shockwave.

It collided with the shadow vortex.

For a heartbeat, the two forces warred. Then everything detonated.

The explosion was so bright that Kade, Evo, Bren, and Tamsin dropped to the ground, arms over their heads, as gold and shadow spiraled through the air like two dragons devouring each other.

The floor collapsed beneath the Wraith King. He clawed his way back up, roaring, but the shadows around him sputtered and failed.

Lira stepped through the smoke, her eyes glowing gold.

"This ends now," she said.

She raised one hand. The conduit opened fully. The shards inside her harmonized, a single pure tone vibrating through the chamber.

A beam of golden annihilation burst from her hand, spearing the Wraith King through the chest.

He screamed.

The shadows vanished.

The crown shard at his core tore free, streaking across the room and slamming into Lira's chest like a falling star. She gasped and arched back as the fifth shard fused into her body with the others.

A blinding sun-white flare erupted outward.

When it faded, the Wraith King was gone. Only dust remained.

The realm shuddered. Walls crumbled. Floors broke apart. The sky itself, visible through the ruined roof, began to split like torn cloth as the dark magic holding the kingdom together died with its master.

"Go!" Bren yelled. "It's all coming down!"

But Lira did not respond. She staggered once, golden light flickering around her, and then collapsed.

Kade caught her before she hit the ground.

"Lira? LIRA!"

Her eyes were closed. Her breathing was shallow. The conduit dimmed but remained warm.

"We have to move!" Evo shouted as massive cracks tore across the floor.

Tamsin pointed. "There. There's an exit through the southern wall!"

Bren took Lira from Kade and carried her between them as they ran, dodging falling stone, leaping gaps in the collapsing floor, racing through the dying kingdom as the sky above shredded into nothing.

Behind them, the Wraith King's palace collapsed with a thunderous roar.

They did not stop until the last whisper of shadow receded and the cursed land gave way to barren rock and clean wind. Bren lowered Lira to the ground gently.

Kade knelt beside her, brushing hair from her face. "Come on, please..."

Hours passed.

Finally, Lira stirred. Her eyes opened. Golden light shimmered faintly in her irises, then faded.

"Lira?" Kade asked softly.

She blinked at him, confused. Her gaze flicked to Bren, Evo, and Tamsin, then back to him.

"Where... where are we?" she whispered.

Kade's breath caught. "It's okay. We're safe."

She frowned. "Safe from what?"

The four of them exchanged a look of dread. Evo swallowed hard. "Kade... she doesn't remember."

Lira looked down at herself, at the glowing conduit, at the faint hum beneath her skin. Then she looked at Kade, whose face was breaking.

"I'm sorry," she whispered, her voice fragile. "Should I know you?"

Kade closed his eyes. The shards had saved her life. They had united. But the cost was already making itself known.

Lira was alive, but she had lost pieces of herself.

CHAPTER TWENTY-FOUR
The Echo of What Was Lost

Lira sat propped against a smooth boulder, watching the four strangers gather close, though they insisted otherwise. The wind tugged at her hair, carrying a faint metallic scent. Desert air. Broken land. Something both familiar and strange.

Kade knelt in front of her again, careful but aching.

"Lira," he said softly, "we're not lying to you. We've been through all of this together. We have saved each other's lives more times than I can count."

She pulled back slightly, wary. "I... I hear what you're saying. And I believe you think it's true. But I don't know you. I don't remember any of that."

Evo crouched beside him, gentler than usual.

"But you feel the shards, don't you?" he asked. "Inside you?"

Lira hesitated, then nodded.

"Yes. They're... humming. Like they are part of me. Like they have always been." She pressed a hand to her chest, where the shards glowed faintly beneath her skin. "So I know you're not making that part up."

Tamsin offered her the Eye.

"Then maybe this will help. You are the only one it listens to. See what it wants us to see."

Lira stared at the artifact uncertainly, then reached out and took it. The Eye pulsed instantly. A soft glow, a low hum, and then a vision flared into the air above it.

The ancient ruin temple appeared, perched on a mountainside shrouded in mist. It was cracked and overgrown with roots from trees older than kingdoms. The symbol of the crown burned faintly along its entrance.

Lira gasped. The vision tugged at something inside her, something just out of reach.

Bren leaned forward. "It showed us that before. It said it might have answers for how to remove the shards safely, once we had all five."

"It wants us to go there," Kade murmured.

"But why?" Lira whispered.

Before anyone could answer, arrows hissed from the ridge. Evo threw himself over Lira as a volley struck the boulder behind them, stone exploding into shards.

"PALACE HUNTERS!" Bren roared.

They surged from the shadows, clad in sleek armor and cloaks, their insignia glinting. A dozen at least, maybe more. They had been waiting.

Kade drew his sword, meeting the first attacker with a clash of steel. Evo spun, twin daggers flashing. Bren barreled forward, axe swinging. Tamsin's sai sliced through the wrist of a hunter who got too close.

Lira scrambled back, heart racing, but her body reacted before her mind could. Golden heat flickered in her veins. Energy crackled around her fingertips.

A hunter lunged at her. She did not think. She thrust her palm forward. A burst of golden force blasted him clear off his feet and slammed him into the cliff wall.

The others stared, startled.

"You still have your power!" Evo shouted.

"Do it again!" Bren yelled.

The palace hunters regrouped, already forming a new line.

"Kade!" Tamsin shouted. "There are too many. We have to go!"

Kade slashed down another hunter, grabbed Lira's wrist, and pulled. They ran through rock and brush, dodging arrows and stumbling over uneven ground until, finally, the sounds of pursuit faded behind them.

They reached a narrow ravine where the hunters could not easily follow. Breathing hard, they pressed against the stone walls, trying to catch their breath. Lira had her hands on her knees, shaking.

Kade was still holding her arm. His voice was low, strained, breaking. "Lira... look at me."

She did. Something in his expression, relief, terror, longing, struck something deep inside her, something her fractured memories recognized even if she did not understand why.

"You do not remember us," he said, his voice cracking, "but... do you feel anything at all when you look at me?"

She swallowed. "I don't know. I... maybe."

Kade stepped closer.

"Then let me try something."

Before she could question it, before she could brace, he kissed her. Not desperate. Not demanding. But full. Strong. Steady. Like someone who had been holding himself together for far too long.

The moment their mouths met, the shards inside her detonated in a rush of molten gold. Power surged through her chest, up her throat, into her lips, into him. Her hands flew to his shoulders. Her breath caught. Heat blossomed behind her eyes. Images flashed:

Kade gripping her hand at the Frostmade Vault. Kade shielding her from wraithfire. Kade hauling her onto a cliff ledge. Kade smiling at her across a campfire. Kade whispering that she mattered. Kade bleeding. Fighting. Protecting. Choosing her every time. Kade looking at her like she was the one impossible thing in his world worth saving.

Her heart slammed against her ribs. When they pulled apart, she was breathing hard, trembling.

Kade searched her face. "Lira...?"

A tear slipped down her cheek.

"I remember you," she whispered. Her fingers brushed his jaw, soft and awed. "Kade... I remember you."

Relief crashed through him so hard he had to close his eyes. Bren, Evo, and Tamsin exhaled all at once.

Lira looked at them, really looked, and recognition, faint but blooming, lit her eyes.

"I remember all of you," she said quietly. "Not everything. Not all at once. But... it is coming back."

"Alright, I'll kiss her next," Bren announced, taking a step forward. "No," Kade answered with one word, and a look that had him step back without another word.

She pressed her hand to her chest, where the shards pulsed warmly.

"And I know this: whatever waits in that ancient temple... I have to face it."

Kade took her hand. "Then we go there together."

Lira nodded. Her memories were incomplete. Her path uncertain. But she was no longer lost.

CHAPTER TWENTY-FIVE
The Road of Remembering

They left the ravine at first light, following a sun-baked path that twisted through cracked earth and rolling scrub. Morning haze softened the horizon, turning the landscape into something blurred, almost dreamlike.

Lira walked between them, listening to the crunch of their boots and the whisper of the wind. Every breath felt like reaching for a memory she could not quite grasp. The others stayed close, near enough for comfort, but far enough to give her space.

For a long moment, no one spoke.

Then Evo, as always, broke the silence.

"So," he said lightly, "have you remembered any of the heroic stuff yet? Mostly mine, of course. There is a lot of it."

Kade groaned. "Spare her."

"No, this is important historical documentation," Evo insisted. "And I should start with the Ice Cliff Incident."

Lira tilted her head. "That sounds bad."

"Oh, it was," Tamsin muttered.

Evo continued dramatically. "Picture this: I step on what I thought was solid ground. It turned out to be a snow shelf thinner than Bren's patience. The whole thing collapsed. I went flailing off the cliff, arms waving, legs kicking, screaming words I do not even remember."

"You screamed my name," Tamsin reminded him.

"I thought you could catch me," he argued.

"You were twenty feet away!"

Lira laughed softly, and Evo's grin widened.

"Anyway," he said, "I am falling to my doom. Then you grab my wrist, nearly yank my arm out of its socket, and hold on while Bren and Kade haul us back up as if we weighed nothing."

Lira felt warmth flicker in her chest: fear, urgency, the burn of cold wind on her face. A memory.

"I remember... grabbing something," she murmured.

"That was me," Evo said proudly. "You saved my life. Do not forget that part."

Bren cleared his throat. "If we are listing rescues, I have one to share."

Tamsin rolled her eyes. "Of course you do."

"No, this one matters," he insisted. He stepped beside Lira, his axe resting across his shoulder.

"After we escaped the Frostmade Vault," he began, "we barely made ten steps into the open before that ice wraith came down out of nowhere. The thing grabbed you around the waist and tried to drag you into the sky."

Lira's breath caught. A flash of cold fingers, weightless fear. She remembered that terror.

"Kade threw a lasso around its middle," Bren said, jerking his chin toward him, "and the four of us hauled the rope with everything we had. It fought like a demon, but we dragged it low enough."

He lifted his axe slightly. "And then I shattered it. One hit. Ice everywhere."

Lira swallowed, her heart beating strangely fast. "I... think I remember the sound."

Bren smiled. "The loudest crack I have ever heard."

Tamsin stepped forward, her grin small and mischievous.

"My turn. The griffin."

Lira frowned slightly. She remembered heat. Wind. Feathers.

"You climbed down to that nest," Tamsin said, "and Bren, Evo, and I nearly tore our arms out holding the ropes steady for you and Kade. You found the shard. Everything was fine until the griffin came back."

Warmth bloomed in Lira's palms, sun-heated wind whipping against her face, talons slicing the air.

"You blasted it," Tamsin said, awe softening her voice. "Golden power everywhere. It screeched and veered off, wings smoking from the hit. But it did not die. It flew away."

Lira felt relief she had not known she needed. "Good."

"Good?" Evo snorted. "It almost killed you!"

"It was just protecting its nest," she said.

Kade, quiet and steady as always, finally spoke as they crested a rise.

"I have one," he said softly. "A memory I think you should know."

Lira slowed, meeting his eyes.

"The serpent," he said, voice low. "The first shard we had to collect."

Her heart thumped.

"You did not just fight it," Kade said. "You used the Eye. You saw straight through its chest, saw the shard trapped inside its heart. And when it reared up to crush you..."

He exhaled slowly, emotion tightening his jaw.

"I held you," he continued. "I held you steady while you reached into it with the shard's power. You tore the shard out from the inside. The creature fell dead at our feet."

Lira's hand rose instinctively to her sternum. "I... remember the pain. And you shouting."

"I was shouting at the serpent," Kade said quietly. "Not at you."

Something warm and fragile fluttered in her chest.

The rest of the day passed in fragments of memory: shared jokes, ruined meals, Tamsin's complaints about sleeping on hard rocks, Evo's dramatic reenactments of every minor battle. Piece by piece, the emptiness inside Lira felt less hollow.

As the sun dipped lower, the land around them began to change. The grass thinned, stones grew larger and older, etched with lines like ancient script. Twisted trees rose in the distance, their branches heavy with moss.

Then the world opened.

Between two crumbling monoliths lay a wide stone staircase descending into golden mist.

The temple.

The same one the Eye had shown her.

Its pillars leaned with age, wrapped in vines thick as ropes. Sunlight slanted through drifting dust, illuminating faint symbols carved along the doorway.

A humming filled the air, deep, resonant, ancient, vibrating straight into Lira's bones.

She stepped forward, breath catching. "I... feel something."

"The shards?" Bren asked.

"Or the place recognizing her," Evo murmured.

Kade stood beside her. "Either way... we're here."

For the first time since waking, Lira felt certain.

"Let us find out what it wants to tell us," she whispered.

Together, they crossed the threshold into the ancient temple, their shadows stretching long behind them as they walked toward the truth waiting inside.

CHAPTER TWENTY-SIX
Into the Temple of the First Crown

The temple rose from the jungle like the bones of some long-dead titan. Its pillars stood cracked by centuries, strangled by thick coils of vine, and a faint hum of ancient magic threaded through the air like a warning. When the First Crown had been reforged into the Crown of Echoes and the Five Kingdoms were born, this temple had been sealed and abandoned.

Its creators vanished from history without a trace.

The jungle claimed the structure in their absence, swallowing stone beneath root and moss, as though the world itself wished to forget what had been built here.

The Eye pulsed softly in Lira's hand as they crossed the threshold. Each beat echoed the rhythm of the five shards thrumming beneath her skin. A faint shiver passed through her.

Pieces of me I still cannot reach. But they are in there.

Kade stepped beside her and rested a steadying hand on her shoulder. "Stay close. There is no telling what this place wants."

They moved deeper.

The first corridor opened into a vaulted passage carved with murals that covered every inch of stone. Time had not dulled their precision. Crowns of light flared above kneeling warriors. Swirling sigils wound across the walls, identical to those etched upon the shards embedded in

Lira's chest. The air felt ancient and oppressive, as though the temple exhaled slowly around them.

"Eyes up," Bren muttered. "This place is built to kill."

He was right.

Evo's boot barely grazed a pressure tile before darts hissed from hidden slits in the walls. He recoiled with a curse, twin daggers flashing as he deflected the first volley. Sparks scattered as steel met steel. Tamsin seized Lira's arm and pulled her behind a pillar while Bren charged forward, his axe raised high. With a roar, he brought it down upon the mechanism concealed within the stone. The trigger shattered, and the darts fell silent.

Evo slid his daggers back into their sheaths and exhaled. "Effective. Brutal. I approve."

They advanced with greater caution after that.

Hall followed hall, each more suffocating with history and expectation. The carvings grew increasingly intricate. They depicted the forging of the Crown of Echoes, five shards bound within a single host. The host was chosen by prophecy. The host was altered. In one mural, a figure stood engulfed in blinding light until no trace of mortal form remained.

Lira stopped before it, her breath shallow.

"Is that meant to be me?" she asked quietly.

Tamsin brushed her fingers across the mural's chipped edge. "Or it is someone who came before you. Prophecies repeat themselves. They do not always end the same way."

"But they might," Lira said. The empty spaces in her memory throbbed like bruises she could not see.

Kade stepped closer, his voice low and firm. "No wall decides your fate. We do."

His hand hovered near hers. She did not move away.

They pressed onward.

The Maze Hall forced them apart. Stone walls shifted with grinding groans, forming patterns designed to confuse and disorient. Evo's curses echoed through false corridors. Bren attempted to break through a barrier and earned nothing but a bruised shoulder for his trouble. Tamsin traced invisible arcs in the air with her sai, studying angles and symmetry until the labyrinth yielded to her logic.

Lira closed her eyes and reached for the faint glow beneath the stone. Sigils shimmered across the walls, barely visible. The shards within her vibrated in response, resonating like tuning forks. She followed that resonance, guiding herself through the shifting paths. One by one, the sealed doors unlocked. The five of them reunited at the far end of the hall.

Beyond it lay a vast circular chamber.

The walls spiraled inward with carvings that represented the five shards. Each spiral converged upon a dais at the chamber's center. Atop it stood a pedestal shaped like an open hand. Resting upon the stone palm lay a book formed of carved tablets, its pages etched with golden sigils that now glowed in answer to the marks burning across Lira's skin.

The air throbbed with restrained power.

Evo stepped forward, awe plain on his face. "That is not subtle."

"It's a ritual chamber," Tamsin said, her voice hushed. "Runic channels. Conduits for energy. This place was built to transform something."

"Or someone," Kade replied.

Lira approached the pedestal slowly. Heat radiated from the stone tablets. The sigils shifted as if alive. When she raised the Eye, the chamber responded. Channels carved into the floor ignited one by one, forming a radiant ring of gold around the dais.

The words etched upon the tablets rearranged. The Eye translated them in a whisper that echoed inside her mind:

When the crown is five, return it to the forge.

When the vessel falters, the temple restores.

The host holds the shards, but not forever.

Give willingly, or be unmade.

Her breath caught in her throat.

Bren rubbed the back of his neck. "Does that tell us how to remove the shards from you?"

"Not exactly," Lira replied. "It says the crown can be reforged here. But if the vessel falters, the temple restores. I don't know whether that means healing or replacing."

"It means we are close," Kade said. "We find the forge. Then we decide what happens next."

Heat surged beneath Lira's skin. The shards pulsed in unison. All five. All within her. The realization struck with such force that her knees nearly buckled.

Kade caught her elbow. "Steady."

She nodded, though unease coiled in her stomach.

Their future was carved into these walls, written in warnings and fire. Every path forward felt perilous.

"Let's rest," Tamsin suggested gently. "Tomorrow we decipher the rest. We face it together."

Together.

Lira inclined her head, yet her gaze remained fixed upon the final line glowing faintly upon the stone.

Give willingly, or be unmade.

Deep within her chest, the shards pulsed in quiet accord, as if they already understood what choice awaited her.

CHAPTER TWENTY-SEVEN
The Forging of the Crown

Morning light filtered through the temple's shattered ceiling, turning the drifting dust into suspended gold. Lira stood at the edge of the ritual chamber with her arms wrapped tightly around herself while the others spread across the carved walls and ancient tablets. The Eye rested in her palm, hovering just above her skin, silent and watchful.

Kade traced a finger along a spiral of sunbursts etched deep into the stone. "These markings match the ones in the floor," he said. "The ones circling the forge."

Tamsin paced around the central dais, studying the inlaid channels of gold that threaded through the stone like veins. "And these runes all speak of a vessel surrendering the shards," she said. "The key word is 'willing.' It appears again and again."

Bren folded his arms and frowned. "So if she does not want to let them go, things become dangerous?"

"More than dangerous," Evo replied, pointing toward another tablet set into the wall. "This one says the temple 'undoes the vessel.' I do not think that promises anything gentle."

Lira swallowed. The Eye felt heavier in her grasp. "Then it is fortunate that I want to give them up."

Kade looked at her, and though his expression softened, the worry in his eyes did not fade. "We are not losing you again," he said quietly. "Not to lost memories. Not to this temple. Not to magic that believes it knows better."

"I'm not going anywhere," Lira whispered. "Not after everything we have endured."

Together they returned to the forge, an ancient metal basin carved into the floor and encircled by a sprawling sigil. A perfect ring of geometric symbols and coiling runes surrounded it, etched so precisely that they seemed almost alive. The air above the design hummed with anticipation. Lira handed the Eye to Tamsin.

The moment Lira stepped inside the circle, the air shifted.

Her shards stirred within her like creatures waking from a long sleep.

Tamsin raised the Eye. Its glow intensified and swept across the chamber as though it were reading the stone itself. One by one, the runes in the floor ignited, light spreading outward in a golden ripple.

Evo let out a low whistle. "I would call that confirmation."

Lira stood at the heart of the sigil. The ancient power vibrating beneath her feet matched the rhythm of her pulse. She closed her eyes and drew in a slow, steady breath. She remembered every time the shards had saved her life, reshaped her strength, and nearly destroyed her.

Then she exhaled.

"I am ready," she said.

The shards flared in response, five bright pulses of power deep within her chest. They were bound to her heartbeat, her breath, and her memories. At first they resisted, clinging to her like frightened spirits.

"It must be willing," Kade reminded her gently. "You must release them. You cannot force them away."

She nodded.

Carefully, deliberately, she loosened her hold.

Warmth flooded her veins, then sharpened into streaks of white fire that blazed beneath her skin. The chamber filled with a rising hum that grew into a crackling roar. Lira gasped as the shards began to separate from her core, each one lifting from her chest in a radiant beam.

The first shard slipped free.

The second followed, rising in a spiral of light.

The third burst outward in a wave of heat that drove her hair back from her face.

The fourth ascended in a column of shimmering particles that scattered like stars.

The fifth, the Wraith King's shard, tore free last. It flickered with a violent dark-gold flame before the sigil consumed its energy and drew it upward.

When the final shard left her, Lira fell to her knees, but she did not collapse.

She breathed.

Her memories returned in a tidal rush. The battles flared behind her eyes. She felt again the bond that tied her to the others, Kade's arms around her, the shadow of the griffin sweeping over the cliffs, Evo's near fall into the abyss, Bren dragging the ice wraith down in a storm of frost and fury, Tamsin's bright laughter cutting through fear. She felt her own terror and triumph before the serpent, and the crushing force of the Wraith King's power colliding with hers. The entire journey blazed within her, whole and unbroken.

Her tears struck the glowing stone at her knees.

"It is all back," she whispered. "Everything."

The forge roared to life.

Above it, the five shards hovered, then separated cleanly into their original forms. Each fragment shone with pure, piercing light. They spun in widening arcs, then drew together, locking into place with ancient precision, fitting as though guided by a design older than kingdoms.

Light engulfed the chamber.

When it faded, a crown rested within the forge. It was a breathtaking circle of gold and crystal, its five points blazing with power beyond measure.

Bren released a reverent breath. "That is the Crown of Echoes."

Evo's crooked grin returned. "And now it belongs to a band of thieves."

Kade reached for Lira, his hand steady despite the light still shimmering in the air. "How do you feel?"

"Weak," she admitted, rising slowly, "but whole. Truly whole."

Shouts echoed from the corridor beyond the chamber.

Boots struck stone.

Steel flashed in the morning light.

Tamsin swore under her breath. "Palace hunters. They must have followed us."

"They're after the crown," Evo said sharply. "Move."

Bren leapt from the dais, his axe already in his grasp. Kade stepped forward and lifted the crown from the forge. For a heartbeat the power within it sparked fiercely against his palm, but then the glow steadied, as if it had accepted his touch.

"Go," Kade called.

Lira forced her unsteady legs into motion. Tamsin caught her arm and pulled her toward the exit as shadows flooded the chamber. Armed hunters poured in, their armor bearing the royal sunburst crest.

"Stop them," one commander shouted. "Seize the crown. Kill them if you must."

Evo's dagger flew, pinning the man's cloak to a column. Bren crashed into the next three hunters with unrestrained fury. Tamsin disarmed another with swift precision, sending his blade skittering across the floor before he understood what had happened.

Kade wrapped an arm around Lira and drew her close as they slipped past a knot of soldiers.

"Stay with me," he murmured.

"I'm not leaving," she replied.

Together, the five of them fled into the maze of ancient halls, the Crown of Echoes blazing in Kade's grasp and the thunder of pursuit echoing behind them. The temple had granted them the crown. Now they would have to survive long enough to decide what such power demanded of them.

CHAPTER TWENTY-EIGHT
The Crown on the Run

The temple collapsed behind them in a storm of dust and shattering stone.

Bren hit the ground first, rolling and dragging Tamsin with him as Evo sprinted through the doorway. Kade shoved Lira through the archway just a heartbeat before the ceiling gave out, the ancient sigils cracking with a force strong enough to shake the mountain.

They stumbled into the sunlight, coughing, bruised, and half-blinded. But they were alive. And they had the crown.

Kade kept one arm around Lira even after they stopped moving. She trembled, her chest aching where the shards had been pulled free, leaving her pale and unsteady. He handed her the crown.

"I've got you," he murmured, his voice low and fierce. "I'm not letting go."

She leaned into him, not out of weakness, but because it felt safe. Real. Anchored. Something she desperately needed.

Evo rose, scanning the horizon. "No hunters. No pursuit."

"For now," Tamsin muttered, wiping dust from her sai. "They will regroup. And they will be furious that we took the crown from under them."

Bren snorted. "We did not steal anything. We only took what they tried to kill us for."

Lira looked down at the crown in her hands. Whole again. Five shards fused seamlessly into one golden circlet. Something ancient. Something powerful. Something that hummed at the edges of her awareness, as if the shards still remembered her.

Kade squeezed her shoulder. "We know where we are going next."

Lira nodded. "The Priestess of the Royal Peaks," she said softly. "The crown wants to go to her. It showed us that back at the spire."

"And she is the only one who can tell us who the rightful ruler is now," Evo added. "Before every kingdom in the realm tears itself apart trying to guess."

Bren cracked his neck. "Then let's move before those hunters dig themselves out."

They slipped into the winding mountain paths, five travelers and a crown racing against a kingdom that did not yet know its ruler. The world softened around them as they journeyed: stone gave way to meadow, cliffs to rolling green. The crown stayed wrapped and hidden, but its presence tugged at them like an unseen current, guiding their steps north.

Kade walked beside Lira nearly every moment. Sometimes their hands brushed. Sometimes he held her steady when the path narrowed. Sometimes she caught him staring when he thought she was not looking. None of it escaped Evo.

"You two are practically glowing," Evo muttered one evening as they made camp. "Anyone with eyes could see it."

Kade flushed scarlet. "Evo, just shut up."

Lira elbowed him softly. "He is not wrong."

Kade looked at her then, really looked, and for a moment the entire world went quiet.

"Lira," he said, his voice gentle and almost hesitant, "after everything, I do not want to pretend anymore."

He reached for her hand. She let him take it.

Tamsin tossed a stick onto the fire. "Finally."

Bren threw his hands up. "Thank the stars. If you two had kept dancing around each other any longer, I would have thrown you off a cliff just to make you admit it."

Kade shot him a glare. Lira tugged him closer before he could say anything.

"No more pretending," she whispered.

He went silent, very flustered, and completely unguarded.

Two nights later, they reached the river at dusk. It was wide and fast-flowing, its surface painted gold by the fading sun.

Lira felt it first. A prickle across her skin. A hollowness in the air. A quiet too absolute.

"Kade," she whispered, "we are not alone."

He reacted instantly. Everyone froze. Weapons drawn. Eyes scanned the brush along the riverbank.

A figure stepped into view. Not a hunter. Not a wraith. Not a creature of shadow or stone.

A man in royal riding leathers. A crimson cloak pinned with the sunburst crest. A polished sword at his hip. His face was young, handsome, and severe.

Prince Wayland. The queen's only child. The heir who never received the crown.

Kade swore under his breath. "Of all the cursed, "

Wayland raised a hand with effortless ease.

"Please," he called across the water, "do not run. My hunters have grown quite tired of chasing you."

Tamsin spat. "Then perhaps they should stop failing."

Wayland's smile was thin and cold. Not amused, not angry, just deliberate and chilling.

"The crown," he said, his eyes locking onto Lira, "belongs to me."

Lira stepped forward, her pulse hammering in her ears. "Your mother shattered the crown. The priestess is meant to determine the next ruler, "

"Yes," Wayland interrupted smoothly. "Well... that did complicate things. She was never supposed to break the crown." His face betrayed no emotion. "I did not hire the assassin to destroy it."

Silence fell over the river like a sudden storm.

Kade stiffened. "What did you just say?"

Wayland's voice remained calm, disturbingly calm. "The assassin's task was to kill my mother. Nothing more. Her destroying the crown was an inconvenience."

Lira felt her blood run cold.

"But he said, 'For the Wraith King!'" Bren growled. "Lira saw it with her own eyes."

"Yes," Wayland said lightly. "That was the point."

Evo's eyes widened in disbelief. "You staged it. So everyone would blame him."

"And while the kingdom turned on a false enemy," Wayland said with a shrug, "I would reveal the intact crown and claim my rightful throne."

Lira's voice dropped to a whisper. "And now?"

Wayland stepped onto the stones at the river's edge. His gaze sharpened, hungry and merciless.

"Now," he said, "you hold the crown I need. And I intend to retrieve it."

Kade moved instantly, placing himself between Lira and Wayland. The prince only smirked.

"By all means," Wayland said, drawing his sword with slow, deliberate precision, "try to stop me."

CHAPTER TWENTY-NINE
The Prince's Claim

The river churned between them, loud and wild, yet the silence that followed Wayland's words felt heavier, more oppressive, than any roar of water.

Kade stepped fully in front of Lira, sword raised, shoulders squared in a stance she had seen him take a hundred times before. He looked ready to die rather than let anyone touch her.

Wayland's mouth curved into a soft, poisonous smile.

"Touching," he said. "Truly. But this," he gestured lazily at Kade, "is not going to stop me."

Evo twirled a dagger between his fingers. "You would be surprised," he said.

Wayland sighed, his eyes narrowing. "I had hoped you would be reasonable. I truly did. I would have even rewarded you for bringing the crown right to me."

"That is not happening," Lira said, tightening her grip on the wrapped circlet at her side.

Wayland's gaze flicked to her. His expression sharpened. "You are the girl," he murmured. "The one who carried the shards. The one who survived them."

He tilted his head, studying her as though she were an object under glass. "You must be extraordinary."

Kade growled. "She is not something you get to examine."

"Oh, I agree," Wayland said. "I plan to kill her, not study her."

Before anyone could react, he lifted his hand. A high whistle cut through the air. Black-fletched arrows shot silently from the brush across the river.

"DOWN!" Kade roared.

Lira felt herself thrown to the ground as arrows splintered the stones where they had been standing moments before. Evo flung a dagger into the undergrowth. Someone screamed and toppled. Tamsin ran toward the riverbank, her sai flashing, knocking aside any arrow that came near. Bren charged forward with his ax, unrelenting.

More hunters emerged from the trees, but these were no ordinary palace hunters. These were elite, armored, disciplined warriors trained for war. They were Wayland's personal guard.

The prince stepped lightly onto the river rocks, his sword gleaming in the sun. "Bring me the crown!" he commanded.

Three armored hunters charged directly at Bren. He met them head-on. His ax smashed through the first shield. The second man staggered before Tamsin slid low, sending him crashing to the ground. Evo darted between them, plunging his dagger into the third's ribs. Steel clashed in a chaotic blur, sparks flying with every strike.

Wayland did not watch the fight. He watched Lira.

Then he moved with impossible speed, so fast she barely saw him. Kade did, and he lunged, intercepting Wayland at the next river stone.

Their swords collided with a violent ring, sparks dancing across the wet rocks.

Wayland laughed, a light, chilling sound. "I wondered if you would be any good," he said.

Kade snarled. "Now you can stop wondering." He shoved Wayland back with a strength born of desperation, the same furious power Lira had seen only when her life had hung in the balance.

Wayland's grin only widened. "Oh, you are angry. Excellent." He attacked.

The river erupted into chaos. Kade met Wayland stroke for stroke, their swords a flurry of steel, water, and breath. Wayland fought like someone trained by the finest palace guard from childhood: clean, precise, lethal. Kade fought like someone who had lived and bled and protected what he could not lose.

Across the river, Bren let out a roar as he smashed two hunters together. Evo twisted away from a spear thrust, cutting the wielder across the thigh. Tamsin used the riverbank for leverage, kicking a hunter into the water.

But more were coming. Dozens more.

Lira clutched the crown to her chest. It vibrated with tension, as if it could sense the violence surrounding them.

Kade stumbled. Wayland's blade sliced across his arm, shallow but enough to draw blood.

"Kade!" she cried.

He forced himself upright, barely steady. Wayland flicked the blood from his sword. "You are strong," he said. "But not strong enough to fight for her. Not anymore." He lunged.

"NO!" Lira screamed.

His gaze slid to her, to the circlet she held. Something inside him shifted, darkened. His resolve sharpened into obsession.

"I will have it," he said quietly. "Even if I have to tear it from your corpse."

He lifted his hand. Every hunter still standing raised their weapons in perfect unison.

Kade stepped in front of Lira without hesitation. "Over my dead body," he hissed.

Wayland's smile thinned. "So be it." He snapped his fingers. The hunters advanced.

Lira backed toward the cliff edge, the drop yawning behind her like the open mouth of a storm.

"Stay back," she shouted. "Or I drop it."

The prince froze. Utterly, terrifyingly still.

"The crown," Lira continued, holding it over the abyss. "If it shatters again, there is no telling how long it will take to find the pieces. The Eye is buried in rubble, maybe even destroyed. All your planning, your mother's death, it will all be for nothing."

A heartbeat passed. Then another. Wayland's mask cracked.

"Step away from that cliff," he said, his voice trembling with restrained rage. "I swear to the gods, if you drop that crown, "

"You will what?" Lira shot back. "Kill me? You already planned that."

The hunters hesitated, glancing at their prince for orders. Wayland lifted a hand to halt them. He could not risk her dropping it. He could not risk losing everything he had already betrayed his kingdom for.

Kade's fingers brushed Lira's back. The others edged closer to his side.

"We need to move," Tamsin whispered.

"Through the cleft," Kade murmured, nodding subtly to the others. He mouthed the word, and Lira nodded. They ran, not toward the prince, not along the path, but sideways into the narrow cleft between two cliffside boulders, a slit most would miss unless desperate. Only by some miracle could Bren fit.

Arrows whistled past them. A hunter shouted. Wayland cursed, his voice breaking with fury. "After them! Bring them back! Now!"

The cleft funneled into a steep slide of gravel and roots. Kade grabbed Lira's wrist, and they half-fell, half-ran down the slope until the river mist swallowed them. The others stayed close behind. Shouts echoed from above. Armor clattered. But the path was too narrow for horses, too uneven for swift pursuit, and the thieves were practiced at escaping in treacherous terrain.

Finally, breathless, they reached the bottom of the ravine, hidden and shielded by rock and shadow. Kade pressed his forehead to hers, hands shaking.

"You insane, brilliant woman," he whispered.

Lira clutched the crown, chest heaving. "I did not know if it would work."

"It worked," he said softly.

Above them, distant and furious, Wayland's roar tore through the valley. The prince was not done. Not even close.

But neither were they. For the first time since the crown left her body, Lira felt something strong enough to steady her: Kade's warm hand over hers, and the knowledge that the real war had only just begun.

Tamsin wiped blood from her cheek. "We need to move."

Evo nodded. "Before he circles around with even more friends."

Bren lifted his ax. "Then let's put as many miles between us and His Royal Murder-y Highness as possible."

CHAPTER THIRTY
The Flight into the Peaks

The cleft narrowed to a jagged throat of stone, forcing them into single file as they pushed through the dim, twisting passage. Every footstep echoed. Every breath sounded too loud. Lira kept glancing over her shoulder, half-expecting Waylen's hunters to emerge from the shadows behind them.

But they did not appear. The prince had truly pulled back for now.

"Keep moving," Kade murmured, guiding her forward with a steady hand on her back. "We need a good two hours between us and the ridge before nightfall."

"Two hours," Bren groaned. "My legs are already full of complaint."

Evo snorted. "Your legs complain about everything, including sitting."

"I sit aggressively," Bren huffed.

Tamsin shook her head. "Both of you shut up. I can still hear hooves in my imagination."

Lira tightened her grip on her pack. The crown's weight felt heavier than ever. Once, the shards inside her had been a strange, burning power. Now they were cold metal, hanging from her shoulder like a reminder she could not escape.

We are taking this to the Priestess, she reminded herself, like the vision had shown. One step at a time.

The cleft eventually spat them out onto a sloping hillside thick with scrub pines and wind-bent stone. The air thinned as they climbed, crisp with the scent of snow melting far above.

Kade scanned the valley behind them. "No sign of them."

"But he will follow," Tamsin said. "A prince does not take humiliation well."

"He'll come back with more men," Evo added. "And better ones."

"We just need to reach the Peaks before he does." Bren shrugged as if that were something simple. "No pressure."

Kade turned to Lira. "How's your head?"

She hesitated. "Still messy. But not as bad as before."

"Your memories are holding?" he asked quietly.

"Mostly," she admitted, looking down. "It's just... some things feel out of order. Foggy. Like I lived two versions of the same moment."

Kade nodded, jaw tight. "If anything feels wrong, tell me."

"I will," she said, though she was not sure she would. Not yet. Not until she understood herself.

They climbed until the valley below became only a distant smear of green and silver. The sun dipped low, painting the peaks in pale gold. At last, they reached a flat patch of ground sheltered by a leaning outcrop. Kade called a halt.

"We'll rest here," he said.

Bren dropped his pack with a groan. "Bless the mountains."

Evo began gathering wood. "We will need a fire. It gets cold up this high."

"I'll set traps," Tamsin said, adjusting her sai. She slipped silently into the trees, her steps soundless.

Lira sank onto a fallen log, exhaustion pulling at every limb. Her hands throbbed, her legs trembled, and her heart still pounded from the fear of the cliff.

Kade crouched in front of her. "You should not have had to do that."

She blinked at him. "Do what?"

"Stand on that cliff," he said, voice low but fierce.

"I had to," she said softly. "He wanted the crown. His hunters outnumbered us. If I hadn't, "

"You could have slipped. Or they could have rushed you." Kade's jaw clenched.

Lira exhaled, a warmth spreading through her chest. "You were scared for me?"

"Of course I was." His voice was rough, unguarded. "I have been scared for you since the moment we left the Guild of Thieves. You're, "

He stopped himself.

She leaned closer. "I'm... what?"

Kade looked away, rubbing the back of his neck. "Important."

Lira smiled faintly. "To the world?"

"To me," he whispered.

Her breath caught.

Before either of them could act on the weight of his words, Evo strolled by carrying firewood.

"Break it up, lovebirds," he said casually. "Try flirting after camp is made. Preferably when I'm not starving."

Kade shot him a murderous look. Lira's cheeks warmed, but she didn't move away from Kade. Not even a little.

Night fell quickly. The fire crackled and sent sparks dancing into the darkness. Bren snored, sprawled across half the camp without shame. Evo sharpened his daggers, while Tamsin prowled through the shadows like a restless cat.

Lira wrapped herself in her cloak, staring up at the peaks rising like jagged teeth against the stars.

"You're thinking too loud," Kade said as he settled beside her.

"I did not know that was possible," she admitted.

"For you, anything is possible."

She elbowed him lightly. "Stop that."

"Stop what?" he asked with a sly smile.

"Saying things that make my heart do strange things," she whispered.

He gave her a small, rueful grin. "Then stop looking at me like that."

She tilted her head. "Like what?"

"Like you're deciding if you're going to kiss me."

Her whole face went hot. "I am not, "

"Lira." He leaned closer, his voice barely above a whisper. "You do not have to be afraid of this."

That soft tone, more than the words themselves, made something inside her crack open.

"I am not afraid," she whispered back.

He touched her cheek gently. The firelight danced across his face. For a moment, she let herself imagine leaning in, closing the inch between them, pressing her lips to his, and letting the world fall away.

"Someone is coming." Tamsin's low warning cut through the moment.

Kade sprang to his feet, sword drawn. "Hunters?"

"Just one," she said. "A scout, perhaps. Far off, but heading this way."

Evo cursed. "Waylen is regrouping."

Bren sat up, hair wild. "We move at dawn. No exceptions."

Lira rose, clutching her pack. The crown shimmered faintly through the leather. The Priestess of the Royal Peaks, she thought. She will know who the crown belongs to. She will know how to end this.

Kade stepped beside her. "Are you ready?" he asked.

She met his eyes. "Yes."

Because even with fear clawing at her ribs, she was not walking this path alone.

CHAPTER THIRTY-ONE
The Ascent to the Royal Peaks

Dawn never truly broke in the high mountains. It seeped in pale and cold, turning the sky a muted gray. By the time the first thin rays touched their camp, Kade was already awake, sharpening his sword in slow, steady strokes. Lira stirred at the scrape of steel and the bite of frost in the air.

"Up," Bren grumbled, stamping warmth into his boots. "The mountains aren't going to climb themselves."

"Give them time," Evo yawned, stretching so wide that his jaw popped. "They seem hostile enough to try."

Tamsin returned from her final perimeter sweep, her breath misting in front of her. "The hunter scout never doubled back during the night. But the trail he left points downhill. He went to report."

Kade nodded grimly. "Then Waylen is on the move."

Lira tightened the straps of her pack. She could feel the crown inside, a weight she carried for the world and for the woman she had once been.

"We leave now," Kade said. "The Priestess is two days' climb from here, if the weather holds."

Evo glanced at the cloud-choked peaks and raised an eyebrow. "Define holds."

Kade did not answer. He did not need to.

The path steepened quickly. A narrow ribbon carved into the mountainside forced them to move in careful lines. Wind clawed at their cloaks, tugged at their hair, and stole breath from their lungs. Lira leaned forward into it, pushing step after step.

Bren trudged behind her, his ax strapped to his back, muttering, "If the Priestess doesn't crown someone after all this, I'm crowning myself."

Evo snorted. "I'd pay to see that."

"You wouldn't survive long enough to see the coronation," Tamsin called from ahead. "You trip over your own feet more than the actual terrain."

Evo put a dramatic hand to his chest. "I am nimble."

"You are chaos with shoes," Tamsin corrected.

Lira smiled despite the cold biting at her cheeks.

Kade dropped back slightly, walking close enough that his shoulder brushed hers for warmth. "How's the breathing?" he murmured quietly so only she could hear.

"Fine," she said, though her lungs burned. "I'm more worried about the ridge ahead."

He followed her gaze. The stone path narrowed until it was barely a ledge. Beside it, an abyss plunged straight down into clouds.

"Stay close to me," he said.

"I always do," she replied, smiling softly.

His expression softened with something unguarded, protective, and aching. But he did not speak further.

They reached the ridge at midday. Snow dusted the stone, thin but treacherous. The mountain wind struck them full force, an icy blast that nearly knocked Bren sideways.

"By all the gods," he swore, flattening himself against the wall.

"Move," Kade commanded, his voice steady against the gale. "One at a time. Keep three points of contact. And do not look down."

"Don't say that!" Evo yelped.

Tamsin went first, her steps small and precise. Evo followed, clinging to the rock like a terrified lizard. Bren muttered a fresh string of curses as he edged forward.

Once they were halfway across, Kade turned to Lira. "You and me."

She nodded, swallowing her fear.

The wind shoved at her immediately, tilting the world and roaring around them. She felt Kade's hand close around hers, firm and grounding.

"I've got you," he said.

Together they stepped along the frozen ledge, boots sliding and fingers numb. Halfway across, a gust slammed into them hard enough to wrench Lira's foot free. She gasped as her balance tipped.

Kade yanked her against him and braced them both against the wall.

"Lira, look at me."

She did.

His forehead rested against hers, breath warm despite the cold. "You're not falling," he said. "Not while I'm here."

Her shaking eased. She nodded. "Okay."

They finished the crossing pressed together, moving as one.

The path beyond widened again, giving them room to breathe. Tamsin scanned the sky with a frown. "We're not alone."

Evo stiffened. "Hunters?"

"No." She pointed.

Far across the valley, dark silhouettes moved along a lower slope. They were small but unmistakably human.

"Ahead of us," Bren said. "They're trying to cut us off."

"Waylen must have split his forces," Kade muttered. "He's learning."

"And getting closer," Lira whispered, feeling the weight of the crown dig into her spine.

Kade touched her arm. "We'll reach the Priestess first. We have to."

They continued climbing higher, colder, and thinner.

By late afternoon, the mountain revealed its second danger. The wind died suddenly, and an eerie silence settled over the slopes.

Evo frowned. "That's never a good sign."

A rumble rolled through the stone beneath their feet. Then another.

Tamsin's eyes widened. "Avalanche."

Kade shouted, "Move!"

Snow exploded above them, a roaring wall of white. Bren grabbed Tamsin and shoved her forward. Evo sprinted ahead. Kade seized Lira's hand and pulled her along as the mountain roared and the world turned to thunder.

"Into the cut!" Tamsin shouted, pointing toward a narrow crevice in the rock.

They sprinted, boots slipping, snow hammering down around them. Lira stumbled, but Kade hauled her upright without breaking stride. Bren barreled forward like a battering ram, carving a path through the falling ice.

The avalanche hit the slope just behind them, devouring the trail they had crossed. They dove into the crevice at the last possible moment. Snow roared past the opening, a white river shaking the stone walls.

They huddled together, breathless, pressed into the narrow shelter. When the rumble finally faded, Lira realized her hands were shaking violently.

Kade covered hers with his. "You okay?"

She nodded, though she was not entirely sure. "That was close."

"Too close," Tamsin said.

Bren let out a shaky laugh. "If this Priestess doesn't offer us a hot meal and a bed of clouds, I'm protesting."

Evo wiped snow from his face. "We're alive. I'll take that."

Kade wasn't looking at any of them. He was staring at the broken trail behind them, the mountain pass now buried under tons of snow.

"They won't follow us," he said. "Not through that. But they will take the lower pass. We still need to beat them to the summit."

Lira gripped the strap of her pack, her heart pounding in her chest. She wanted to collapse, to sleep, to cry, but instead she forced herself to speak. "Let's go."

Kade met her eyes. "Right behind you," he murmured.

Together, they pressed on, the cold wind tugging at their cloaks and the peaks towering above them like ancient judges. They moved toward the hidden sanctuary of the Priestess, unaware that the mountains held secrets of their own.

CHAPTER THIRTY-TWO
The Calling of the Crown

The climb into the upper pass felt less like a trail and more like a trial. Snow swirled in thin, ghostlike ribbons, and the wind whistled between jagged stone spires that rose like the ribs of an ancient beast. Lira kept one hand on the pack holding the reformed crown, its weight somehow heavier than before.

Ahead, the path ended at a carved archway in the mountainside. Smooth ice, shaped by old magic, glowed faintly with symbols Lira did not recognize.

Evo let out a low whistle. "If this is the front door, I'm scared to see the foyer."

Tamsin elbowed him sharply. "Shut it."

They stepped beneath the arch.

The air stilled instantly. The wind died, the cold softened, and even their breathing seemed muted.

Then a figure emerged from within. A tall woman draped in layered white and pale silver, her hair braided with frost crystals that did not melt. Her eyes were not human eyes, they were too old, too clear, like two winter moons.

The Priestess of the Royal Peaks.

She looked at each of them in turn. When her gaze reached Lira, it passed over her, not dismissively, but purposefully, as if Lira were a doorway, not the destination.

The Priestess's breath hitched just once when her gaze reached Kade. Then she bowed her head. Not a polite inclination, but a full lowering, to a ruler.

Kade froze. "I, Priestess, I think you, "

Her voice cut through him like ice breaking. "At last."

Evo blinked. "At last... what?"

The Priestess lifted her eyes to Kade. "The mountains have whispered your name for two decades, child of Karthen."

Kade staggered back. "Kar...then?"

Lira's heart slammed against her ribs. Karthen. Not a dead kingdom. A living realm.

The Priestess stepped closer, every movement as fluid as drifting snow. "You were taken as a young boy, barely out of your cradle. Hidden. Lost to memory and magic. But not to blood. Not to destiny."

"I'm not, " Kade's voice cracked. "I was an orphan. I grew up on the Lower Quarter docks. I don't know anything about Karthen, or royalty, or, "

"You know your name," the Priestess whispered. "You kept that, even stripped of all else."

Kade swallowed. "Kadeon."

She nodded. "Kadeon Vereth Karthen. Firstborn son and only heir to the royal family of the kingdom of Karthen."

Silence crashed over the group like an avalanche.

Bren sucked in a breath. "His parents... they're alive?"

The Priestess's gaze softened. "Very much alive. Searching still."

Lira felt her knees weaken. Kade's parents. His home. He had not been abandoned. He had been stolen.

The Priestess turned to Lira for the first time, her expression unreadable. "And you," she murmured, "Bearer of the Shard of Choosing."

Lira swallowed. "I, I didn't choose it. It forced itself into me."

"Because it recognized you," the Priestess said, lifting a pale hand. "Not as the ruler, but as his anchor. His destiny. The one soul who could safely carry the shard meant for him until the time of the claiming."

Time slowed. Lira could not breathe.

Kade's voice was barely a rasp. "The queen... she shattered it. Can you tell us why?"

"Because she feared the crown would pass to her son," the Priestess replied, her eyes turning as cold as the mountain stone. "She knew her bloodline could inherit. She shattered it at her death to force a new Choosing, something she believed she could manipulate."

Bren snarled. "So the kingdom is in chaos because she did not want her son to rule?"

"Yes," the Priestess said simply. "The crown selects the next ruler. And it has already chosen one."

Her gaze found Kade again. A tremor ran through him, fear, recognition, and something else, deeper, older.

Lira stepped closer, unable to help it. His hand brushed hers, seeking. She laced her fingers through his.

The Priestess watched them, her expression shifting with quiet, ancient approval.

"You were chosen together," she said. "A king and the one fate bound him to."

Kade's breath shuddered. "I didn't ask for this."

"Destiny does not require permission," the Priestess replied. "It requires only courage."

She turned toward the open entrance of the Sanctuary, a vast cavern glowing with blue fire.

"The crown awaits," she said. "Come, Kadeon Vereth Karthen. Let the mountains recognize their king."

Kade's fingers tightened around Lira's. She squeezed back, steadying him, grounding him, even as her own heart splintered and reshaped itself.

"Go," she whispered. "You're not alone."

He nodded.

Together, they stepped into the Sanctuary, toward the Choosing, toward his truth, and toward the future the crown had waited twenty years to reclaim.

CHAPTER THIRTY-THREE
The Sanctuary of the Royal Peaks

The Sanctuary was not a cavern. It was a cathedral carved by time and magic.

The walls rose in spirals of ice and stone, reflecting soft blue fire that hovered in the air like weightless lanterns. Symbols glimmered along the walls, long, ribbon-like marks in ancient script. Some glowed warm gold, some cold silver, and one color Lira had never seen before: a deep midnight blue streaked with pale white veins.

Power.

Old power.

Older than kingdoms.

Older than the crown itself.

The Priestess moved ahead of them without a sound, her robes whispering across the frost-glass floor.

"The trials await," she said.

Kade's hand trembled in Lira's, though his voice did not, when he whispered, "I'm ready."

Lira squeezed his fingers once more, then let go. The moment their hands separated, the blue flames brightened, flaring as if drawing in breath.

The Priestess turned to the others. "Only the chosen heir may enter the Rings of Claiming."

Evo muttered, "Rings? As in plural?"

"Three rings," she said. "Three truths. Three proofs."

Bren whistled low. "Sounds like a party."

Kade swallowed hard. "And Lira?"

The Priestess looked at Lira with an unreadable expression. "She will stand where the Shard-bearer must, at the Threshold."

Lira felt the words like a cold wind down her spine. "The Threshold?"

The Priestess nodded. "Where the fate of the heir's heart is weighed."

Kade turned sharply toward her. "I don't like the sound of that."

The Priestess only motioned him forward. "Begin the trials, Kadeon Vereth Karthen. Your crown awaits."

He hesitated long enough for his eyes to meet Lira's. Then he stepped forward.

The instant his boot crossed the first glowing circle inscribed in the floor, the Sanctuary came alive. Light flared. Air shifted. The walls themselves hummed. The first trial had begun.

The first ring was the Ring of Courage.

The blue flames spiraled into a vortex and coalesced into an enormous shape, shadow made solid. A beast formed of mountain-storm and winter-night, all teeth, sweeping antlers, and ink-black hide that seemed to swallow the light. A Guardian Beast of the Peaks.

Lira gasped and reached forward, only to strike an invisible barrier. The Threshold. She could see Kade but could no longer reach him.

"Kade!" she cried.

He did not back away. He drew his sword with steady, deliberate movements, his breath clouding in front of him.

The creature lunged.

The fight was brutal and primal, all instinct and strength. Kade rolled beneath a crashing antler strike, brought his blade up, and scored the beast's flank. Frost exploded across the floor. He ducked again, slid between the creature's legs, and came up behind it, driving his blade deep between its ribs.

Light burst outward. The beast dissolved. The First Ring ignited in bright gold.

Kade stepped into the next circle: the Circle of Truth.

This time, no monster rose. Instead, the Sanctuary shimmered, and Lira's breath caught.

A small boy appeared. Dark hair. Bare feet. Dirty clothes. Big, terrified eyes.

Kade froze. It was him. Before the docks. Before the Lower Quarter. Before the memory loss. A smaller version of himself, crying in the corner of a dim room, calling for a mother he had long forgotten.

Kade fell to his knees.

"I... I don't remember you," he whispered to the child. "But I'm here. I'm right here."

The boy looked at him, his small hands trembling.

"Are you coming back for me?"

Kade's eyes filled with tears. "I'm sorry. I didn't know how. I didn't know who I was."

The boy lifted a tiny hand.

Kade took it gently. "But I will not leave you again."

Light flared from their joined hands. The child dissolved into gold motes that spiraled around the ring.

The Second Ring ignited.

The Priestess exhaled softly. "The final truth."

Kade stepped into the third circle, the Circle of Worthiness.

This time, the light gathered and formed Lira.

Perfect. Exact. But not her.

This Lira was clad in gold flame. Her hair drifted like smoke, and her eyes shone with shard-light she no longer possessed. She was a Lira of destiny, not of reality.

Kade flinched. "This isn't her," he said.

The spectral Lira spoke with a voice that was Lira's, yet older, more knowing.

"Will you choose a crown," she asked, "if it means losing her?"

Kade's breath stilled.

The real Lira's heart plummeted.

"No," he whispered.

"Will you choose a kingdom," the apparition pressed, "if it means walking its halls alone?"

Kade shook his head. "I will not rule by sacrifice."

"Then you choose wrong," the spirit said, raising a hand of golden fire toward him.

Lira screamed, "KADE!"

But he did not retreat. He stepped forward.

"If ruling costs me her, then I do not want the crown," he said, his voice steady. "And I am not worthy of it."

The spirit froze.

The gold fire faded.

The apparition bowed. "You are a true king," it said.

The Third Ring ignited.

The crown descended. Light pooled around Kade like liquid dawn, the three rings turning in slow, deliberate orbit. Gold for the line of kings, silver for the chosen protector, midnight-blue for destiny itself.

Every breath in the chamber stilled. Even the mountain winds outside fell silent.

The Priestess's voice echoed like a chorus of bells. "Kadeon Vereth Karthen, chosen of the Crown, kneel."

Kade lowered himself to one knee, palms open, head bowed. Lira felt her throat tighten. Not with jealousy, not with fear, but with an aching, soul-deep rightness. She had carried the shard because it had always been meant for him. She had been shaped, forged, and guided to him. His destiny, as the Priestess had said.

The crown tilted downward.

Then the mountain's outer doors slammed open.

A violent gust tore through the sanctuary, scattering embers and whipping cloaks. The Priestess did not move, but her guards shifted instantly. Tall, masked figures carved of white stone and shadow stood ready, hands resting on weapons that hummed faintly with power.

Bootsteps thundered across the chamber.

Prince Waylen of Ylaria strode into the light, helm under one arm, fury burning in his storm-gray eyes. Behind him stood half a dozen elite royal hunters and his personal guards.

His voice cracked through the sanctuary like a blade. "STOP!"

The crown froze in mid-air.

The Priestess turned her head slightly, no more, and the temperature in the room dropped. "You enter sacred ground unannounced."

"I enter to claim what is mine by right." Waylen's gaze cut to Kade. "I am the ruling-age heir of the last bloodline to wear the crown. My mother, Queen Elara, died wearing it. I am alive. I am of age. And by the oldest law carved into these peaks, I may issue the Challenge."

Lira's stomach fell.

The Priestess finally faced him. "You dare invoke it."

"I do." Waylen stepped forward, chin raised. "If the crown chooses a new bloodline while a rightful heir of ruling age still lives, that heir may challenge the chosen one. The victor takes the crown. The defeated yields or dies."

The sanctuary trembled with the weight of his words.

Kade rose slowly to his feet. "So this is what you want? A fight to the death?"

Waylen's eyes were shards of ice. "You would take the rule of the Five Kingdoms from me, a prince born and trained to lead, when you did not even know your own name?"

Lira stepped between them, fury sparking. "He didn't choose to lose his past."

Waylen ignored her. "I issue the Challenge according to ancient law."

The Priestess lifted her staff. The rings around Kade dimmed. The crown hovered motionless, waiting.

Her voice carried the weight of the mountain itself. "Challenge acknowledged."

A ripple of power tore through the air.

Her guards moved as one, forming a perfect line before the crown. Six beings taller than any mortal, their armor flowing like living moonstone. Their weapons flared with glyphs too ancient to decipher.

The Priestess's eyes glowed violet. "The crown is no longer in mortal hands. Until the duel, it shall be held and guarded by me and my guard."

One guard reached out, and the crown floated into his grasp, suspended by an invisible force, untouched by mortal fingers.

Waylen bowed stiffly. Kade clenched his fists. Lira felt a storm building inside her.

The Priestess continued, her voice steady and unwavering. "By law, the Challenge must be public. It shall be held in the Royal Arena, before the five banners. The duel ends when one yields his claim."

Her gaze sharpened like a blade. "Or when one falls."

Silence followed. Heavy. Absolute.

Then the mountain wind carried the echo of horns outside, the horns of the Peaks sounding a message that would travel across kingdoms with frightening speed.

The Priestess lifted her face. "Word has already gone out. The lost prince of Karthen has been found and has been challenged."

She turned her eyes to Kade. "Your family has been notified. They will ride to meet you."

Kade staggered slightly, and Lira saw the tremor in his breath. Everything shifted.

The Priestess lowered her staff. "The Challenge will commence when all five kingdoms gather to witness it."

Waylen smirked triumphantly. Kade squared his shoulders. Lira moved to his side, her hand brushing his.

Bren, Evo, and Tamsin stood silently, waiting for the next move.

And the crown, held by beings who could not be killed and could not be stopped, glowed with a deep, patient power.

The Choosing was not over. It had only just begun.

CHAPTER THIRTY-FOUR
The Descent from the Peaks

The sanctuary doors opened, and the wind of the high peaks swept in, cold enough to sting and sharp enough to bite. The path spiraled downward far below them, a narrow ribbon carved into the mountain's spine. Snow drifted in lazy sheets, and clouds clung to the cliffs like veils.

The Priestess stepped forward first, her moonstone-clad guardians forming a protective circle around the floating crown. Their movements were eerie, silent and fluid, impossible to track. Shadows bent with them, and light shifted unnaturally. As one, they began the descent.

The procession down from the Royal Peaks stretched across the narrow mountain road like strands of enemies forced into the same braid.

At the front walked the Priestess of the Peaks, pale and unearthly, her steps whisper-soft on snow. Behind her, the six towering temple guardians carried the crown, suspended in a cradle of invisible force and glowing faintly with a pulse like a heartbeat.

Behind them followed Kade, Lira, Bren, Evo, and Tamsin. Trailing alongside in formation, close enough to breathe on, marched Prince Waylen, his armored hunters, and a handful of grim-faced royal guards.

The Priestess had declared peace until the Challenge. No one liked the rule, and no one obeyed it gracefully. The tension was thick enough to crack stone.

They had barely gone a hundred paces before one of Waylen's hunters gave a low, mocking whistle.

"Look at that," he said loudly. "The soon-to-be king can barely walk a mountain path without clutching his sword."

Kade didn't look back. "I'm clutching it because your prince keeps staring at me like he wants a kiss. Sorry, I'm taken."

Lira smothered a smile.

Waylen laughed sharply. "If I stare at you, street-king, it would only be because I cannot fathom why destiny chose someone as unremarkable as you."

Evo turned immediately. "Say that again, princeling. I dare you."

One of Waylen's guards spoke instead. "Careful, little man. Your tongue will not help him in the arena."

The Priestess didn't break stride. "Enough," she said. Her voice was calm, yet power laced every syllable. The mountains themselves seemed to listen.

A gust of wind swept down the cliffside, pelting both groups with ice crystals like stinging needles.

Tamsin grinned at Waylen's hunters. "See that? Even the Peaks think you're annoying."

Another hunter sneered. "Funny words from a girl who hid behind the men every time someone lifted a blade."

Tamsin ground her teeth, but before she could respond, Evo muttered loudly, very loudly, "Unbelievable. Two steps into the journey, and I can already smell Waylen's ego."

Tamsin clicked her tongue. "That's not his ego, Evo. That's his armor. It smells like cold metal and disappointment."

Bren snorted. "Pretty sure disappointment is the official crest of Ylaria."

The hunters stiffened. One glared back. "Do you want to say that to our faces?"

Bren spread his hands innocently. "We did. The problem is your faces did not improve it."

A couple of temple guardians actually paused, as if processing humor for the first time in three thousand years.

Waylen rolled his eyes skyward. "Children. I am traveling with children."

Tamsin brightened. "Oh look, he can identify himself."

Waylen's jaw snapped shut after he unintentionally walked into that one.

As they continued downward, Prince Waylen drifted closer to Kade, though he kept several paces between them.

"You stand tall for someone who has no training worthy of the crown," Waylen murmured under his breath.

Kade didn't look at him. "You will see soon enough what training I have."

Waylen chuckled low. "Training you picked up in alleys. Fascinating. Truly."

Bren bristled. "He fought his way out of alleys while you practiced sword forms on polished marble floors with trainers too scared to actually touch you."

"Yes," Waylen replied with a cold smile. "And one of us will be dead soon, so I suppose we will learn whose upbringing was more useful."

Kade's jaw tightened, but he held his ground.

Lira stepped closer, her shoulder brushing against his. It was a silent reminder that he was not alone.

Waylen noticed. "Touching," he said. "Though I have heard destiny pairings rarely survive the Challenge. Something about the strain of watching your chosen risk death?"

Lira kept her gaze on the terrain ahead. "It won't be his death."

"Enough," the Priestess said again. This time, the ground shook beneath their feet.

Both groups fell silent. No one dared test her again for a long while.

Hours passed as they descended into thicker clouds and sharper wind. The path never widened enough to separate the two groups, so they moved in tense formation, every breath charged with anticipation.

Occasionally, the mountain revealed its dangers: a bridge of ice, a narrow ledge with a thousand-foot drop, or the distant roar of an avalanche far below. Each time, the Priestess glided forward, her staff glowing, and the threat dissolved.

Even Waylen grew quiet. For a brief stretch, the only sounds were boots crunching in the snow and the faint hum of the crown held between the Priestess's guards.

Kade finally exhaled. "It is strange."

"What is?" Lira asked.

"That the crown is right there, close enough to touch, yet it feels farther away than before."

Lira nodded. "Tomorrow it can be yours."

"Tomorrow," he echoed softly, "I could be king. Or dead."

Waylen's voice drifted from behind. "Make peace with both possibilities, Karthen. It will make the arena easier."

Evo barked a laugh. "Bold words for a man nervous enough to sweat in the snow."

Waylen stiffened. "I am not, "

"Your cloak is soaked through," Tamsin said sweetly.

Waylen glared at them all.

The Priestess sighed. She actually sighed. "Mortals."

They descended a steep switchback, boots scraping against the ice-patched trail. The wind carried the sound of distant horn calls rolling across the valleys, a reminder that kingdoms were stirring and word was spreading.

From somewhere behind, Evo muttered, "Hey, Bren, do you think the prince's cavalry training included learning to march like a stiff tin soldier?"

Bren stage-whispered, very loudly, "No. They teach that on the first day at the Ylarian Academy of the Over-Polished Teacups."

Tamsin responded in theatrically tragic tones. "If only we were wearing our nice cloaks, we could fit in."

One of the hunters barked, "Careful. Keep running your mouths, and the mountain might decide one of you should fall off the side."

Bren did not miss a beat. "With your aim? We're safe."

Even Lira caught herself smiling.

But Waylen snapped, "If you three had any sense of your place, you would stay silent behind your betters."

Bren squinted dramatically at him. "We tried. But they aren't walking in front of us."

A couple of hunters smothered reluctant snorts.

Waylen's glare sharpened. "I was trained by the greatest tacticians alive. You are just gutter rats with lucky mouths."

Tamsin offered sweetly, "Bold words from someone who keeps losing to gutter rats with lucky mouths."

Waylen's lips parted in outrage.

Kade, walking just ahead with Lira, murmured, "You three really do not know how to avoid trouble, do you?"

"No," they said in unison.

"And we never will," Bren added proudly.

One of the guards snorted bitterly. "Sarcasm is their only personality trait."

Bren smiled broadly. "No, no. Sarcasm is an art. You lot are just the canvas."

The hunters glowered. The prince glowered harder.

At the next rest stop, Waylen said flatly, "Just know this. When I win, I will not gloat. I will simply rule as I was meant to."

Evo blinked. "You're planning the post-battle speech already? Wow. Confident."

Bren added, "He must practice in the mirror every morning."

Tamsin chimed in, "Probably with dramatic hair flips."

Waylen's hair actually flipped as he jerked around to glare at them.

As the groups packed up to continue, the Priestess glided between them like an ancient wind.

"The Challenge is sacred," she said sternly. "The journey to it must also be sacred. Hold your anger. Hold your blades. I will bind every tongue here in silence if you do not obey."

All three of Kade's companions clamped their mouths shut. Waylen's hunters went rigid.

As they resumed walking, Kade leaned close to Lira.

"I'm starting to think," he murmured, "that the Priestess did not realize she would be escorting a traveling circus."

Lira smirked. "She's probably regretting her life choices."

Kade's expression softened. "You okay?"

Lira nodded. "As long as you are."

As dusk approached, they reached a plateau where the wind softened and the sky opened above them. Here, the Priestess declared that they would rest.

Her guards planted their staffs in the snow, forming a protective ring around the crown. A pale, shimmering barrier rose from the ground like rippling light.

"None may cross," she warned. "Not even to look closer."

Waylen's gaze lingered on the crown, hungry and desperate. Kade saw it, and Waylen saw that he saw it.

Their eyes locked. No words were spoken. None were needed.

Ahead of them, kingdoms stirred. Families were being alerted. An arena was preparing for a duel that would decide the future of five realms.

But for now, two heirs walked the same mountain path, surrounded by guards, hunters, and an immortal Priestess determined not to let them kill each other.

That night, under the cold glow of a thousand stars, the two future kings sat on opposite sides of the fire. They were surrounded by their allies and united only by the mountain's demand for peace.

CHAPTER THIRTY-FIVE
The Road to Karthen

Dawn rose pale over the plateau and cast a silver wash across the snow packed stones. The camp stirred slowly as both groups woke. Breath misted in the cold air while small fires crackled and travelers gathered their gear for the journey ahead.

At a quiet gesture from the Priestess, the protective barrier around the crown dissolved. The shimmering light sank into the ground like melting frost.

"Today," she announced, her voice carrying easily across the camp, "we leave the mountain path and descend into the lowlands. By nightfall we will meet Karthen's royal escort."

All eyes turned immediately toward Kade.

His breath caught in his throat.

His parents were alive. They were real. They were waiting.

For a moment the wind seemed to quiet around him, as though even the mountain paused to listen.

Lira stepped quietly to his side. She studied his face with careful attention, as if she feared that touching him might shatter the fragile steadiness he had found.

"You don't have to be strong every moment," she murmured.

Kade swallowed hard. "Maybe not. But I need to be strong for this moment."

Waylen swept past them, his cloak snapping sharply in the wind.

"If the long lost prince requires time to compose himself," he said coolly, "I suppose we could delay our departure."

Evo shot him a glare. "Someone woke up on the wrong side of the crown he does not have."

The Priestess raised one hand.

Silence fell instantly. The quiet was sharp and absolute.

"Walk," she commanded.

The procession formed once more.

As they descended from the frozen cliffs, the landscape slowly began to change. The deep snow gave way to frost, and the frost softened into damp earth. Patches of green grass appeared through the thinning drifts while tall pines rose around them. Their branches sagged under the weight of morning dew.

At last the path widened enough for the two groups to separate by a few cautious paces.

It did not widen enough for them to escape each other.

Tamsin nudged Bren with her elbow. "Look at that," she said loudly enough for everyone to hear. "The prince's hunters keep perfect formation even when peeing in the woods."

One of the hunters turned his head and growled, "We can hear you."

"Perfect," Bren replied cheerfully. "I would hate for you to miss such high quality commentary."

Waylen now walked several strides ahead, attempting to reclaim some measure of royal dignity. Instead, he looked increasingly irritated by Kade's presence beside the Priestess at the front of the procession.

One of the hunters muttered under his breath, "You three are insufferable."

Tamsin smiled brightly. "You are welcome."

The Priestess continued forward without speaking. The tight line of her jaw suggested that her vow of peace was being tested severely.

Hours passed as the forest thickened around them. Shadows stretched longer between the trees, and the quiet of the woods settled over the procession like a watchful presence.

Although the banter continued around her, Lira felt a growing weight settle deep within her chest.

Kade noticed.

"You're quiet," he said softly.

"So are you." The wind tugged loose strands of her hair across her cheek.

"I have been thinking," he admitted. "What about you?"

She hesitated before answering. "I have been fearing."

He slowed his pace and glanced at her. "Fearing what?"

"That I will lose you," she whispered, her voice unsteady. "To a crown. To a duel. To a destiny that has already decided too many things."

Kade stopped walking and turned toward her.

Lira nearly collided with him.

He faced her fully, his gaze steady and warm.

"You did not carry the shard for me," he said quietly. "You carried it with me. I am here because destiny chose both of us. That has not changed."

Waylen's voice drifted back from the front of the line.

"If you two have finished whispering sweet nothings, we still have a road to travel."

Lira didn't even lift her gaze toward him. "Jealousy is unattractive."

Waylen sputtered in outrage while several of the hunters behind him struggled to hide their laughter.

Kade pressed his lips together to hide a grin. "Feeling better?"

"A little," Lira admitted.

"Good," he said gently. "Because when all of this is over... I'm not letting you walk away from me."

Her heart skipped at the quiet certainty in his voice.

Waylen made a dramatic gagging sound. Evo immediately mimicked him.

The Priestess's staff began to glow faintly.

"Peace," she warned.

Her tone carried the weary authority of someone whose patience was rapidly fading.

By late afternoon, a deep sound rolled across the forest like distant thunder.

Horns.

Long and metallic, their call echoed through the towering trees.

Bren straightened abruptly. "Either we are about to be trampled by very organized elk, or that is Karthen."

Evo shaded his eyes as he scanned the distant treeline. "If it is elk, we're dead. If it's Karthen, Waylen's pride is dead."

Waylen's jaw tightened. "Mock me all you like. Royal escorts do not frighten me."

"Not the escort," Tamsin replied sweetly. "Your future irrelevance."

Kade's heart began to pound hard against his ribs.

Footsteps echoed through the forest.

Voices followed.

Then came the thunder of hooves.

A column of riders emerged from the trees. Their banners of silver and deep black snapped sharply in the wind. Their armor gleamed like polished obsidian beneath the fading sunlight. Their formation was flawless, disciplined, and unmistakably Karthen.

At the center of the column rode a man and a woman whose presence seemed to command the very air around them.

The King and Queen of Karthen.

Alive.

Real.

His parents stood before him.

Kade felt his knees weaken beneath him. For a moment, the world seemed to tilt. Lira caught his hand before he could stumble and steadied him, but the air would not come easily to his lungs.

The Queen brought her horse to a halt first. Her deep golden eyes filled instantly with tears as she looked at him.

The King dismounted before his horse had even fully stopped. His armor clattered as his boots struck the ground. He stepped forward slowly, staring at Kade as though the world had returned something he had mourned for years.

"Kadeon," he whispered.

The name seemed to shatter the stillness around them.

Kade released a strangled sound that was part sob and part breath as he took a step forward.

Before he could speak, Prince Waylen strode ahead and lifted his voice.

"I greet the royal house of Karthen on behalf of Ylaria."

Neither of Kade's parents acknowledged him.

The King reached Kade first. His hands rose to frame his son's face for a brief, disbelieving moment. Then he pulled him into a fierce embrace.

"My son," he breathed.

"My boy."

Kade clung to him with equal force. Words refused to form. The years of loss and uncertainty had gathered in his chest all at once.

Prince Waylen stood frozen nearby. His jaw hung slightly open as the entire Karthen escort dismounted and dropped to one knee before their returned prince.

While Kade held the parents he had once believed dead, movement stirred within the forest around them. Riders appeared along the distant horizon, emerging one by one through the trees. Their banners rose high above the branches.

Karthen's forces had arrived.

Far beyond them, more banners appeared in the distance. Their colors were unfamiliar. Their symbols belonged to other kingdoms.

The realms were gathering.

The arena was being prepared.

The duel was no longer a rumor whispered in taverns or murmured in royal courts.

It had become a promise.

Destiny was moving forward, and it would not wait forever.

At last, Kade stepped back from his father's embrace. The Queen reached up and gently touched his cheek. Her gaze held both fierce pride and deep sorrow.

"You have us now," she said softly. "You have your home. We will face whatever comes together."

Lira swallowed hard as she watched them.

Because destiny had not finished with Kade.

And neither had danger.

CHAPTER THIRTY-SIX
The Arena of the Five Kingdoms

The procession began to move at a slow and deliberate pace. The moment felt careful and reverent, almost unreal. Karthen's royal horses were brought forward, each one a midnight-coated creature whose dark eyes reflected both ember light and the fading stars. Horses were offered to everyone from both groups for the remainder of the journey.

Their breath steamed in the cold morning air as Kade approached the horse chosen for him.

It was a warhorse, powerful and disciplined, bred for battle and trained with precision. Yet the moment Kade placed his hand against its neck, the animal lowered its ears gently, as though it sensed something within him that he had not yet fully discovered in himself.

His mother smiled softly.

"They know their prince," she whispered.

Prince Waylen scoffed quietly under his breath. "It must be pleasant to have beasts flatter you."

Bren grinned immediately. "Don't be jealous. I'm certain that somewhere a donkey admires you greatly."

Evo leaned closer and lowered his voice. "Or perhaps a goat."

Tamsin spoke with calm certainty. "A blind goat."

Waylen's eye twitched.

Even the King appeared to be struggling to keep a straight face.

When the procession set out again, the forest slowly gave way to rolling hills that shimmered deep green and gold beneath the rising sun. Karthen soldiers rode ahead and behind the company, their banners streaming proudly in the wind.

Kade rode at the center of the procession beside his parents.

For a long while none of them spoke. The silence wasn't uncomfortable. Instead it felt full, heavy with the weight of lost years and the sudden presence of years that might yet be reclaimed.

At last the Queen reached across the small space between their horses and brushed her gloved fingers lightly against Kade's sleeve. The gesture was tentative, as though she needed constant reassurance that he was truly there beside her.

"Kadeon," she said softly, speaking his name as though it carried sacred meaning. "Do you remember nothing at all? Not even a fragment of home?"

"Only my name," he admitted quietly. "Nothing else survived."

His father's jaw tightened.

"We searched for you for years," the King said. "We searched every corner of the kingdom. We believed that you might still be alive somewhere."

The Queen turned her gaze away for a moment and blinked rapidly.

"I prayed for that," she said. "Every single day."

Kade swallowed as emotion tightened his throat.

"I grew up believing I was nobody."

"Never," the King said at once. His voice was deep and fierce. "You were never nobody."

Lira rode just behind them. The weight of that moment pressed painfully against her chest. She lowered her gaze, not wishing to intrude upon their reunion. At the same time, she found that she did not want to drift too far from it.

The Queen noticed her.

"And this," the Queen said gently as she guided her horse slightly to the side, "must be the young woman who carried the shard with you."

Lira nearly lost her breath. "Yes, your Majesty."

"Lira saved my life," Kade said without hesitation.

The Queen's expression softened at once.

"Then she helped save our world as well," the Queen said warmly. "Come. Ride beside us."

Two horses behind them, Waylen made an exaggerated gagging sound.

Evo muttered, "Someone's jealous their mommy isn't proud of them."
Tamsin added thoughtfully, "Perhaps the goat is proud."

The King pretended not to hear the exchange, although he did not entirely succeed.

When the royal couple turned their attention toward Kade's companions, their expressions shifted from formal curiosity to genuine interest.

"And these," the King said carefully, "are your companions?"

"My family," Kade answered simply.

Bren bowed dramatically from horseback and nearly toppled off his saddle in the process.

"Bren of Nowhere, at your service."

"Tamsin," she said with a crisp nod.

"Evo," he added with considerably less grace.

The Queen covered a small smile with her hand.

"Kadeon has certainly kept interesting company."

"We keep him alive," Evo replied.

"And humble," Tamsin added.

"And entertained," Bren finished proudly.

Kade released a quiet sigh. "Unfortunately, all of that is true."

Waylen gave a sharp, derisive snort. "You parade gutter rats before royalty?"

The King looked directly at Kade. His gaze was calm, steady, and weighing.

"Are they loyal?"

"With their lives," Kade replied without hesitation.

His father nodded once. "Then they are welcome."

Waylen looked as though he might actually be sick.

As the procession traveled south, the roads grew steadily busier. Travelers stepped aside when the royal escort approached, dropping to their knees when they recognized the banners of Karthen. Word traveled ahead with astonishing speed that the lost prince had returned.

By the time they reached the main trade roads, caravans from other kingdoms had begun to appear. Bright banners snapped in the wind above ornate wagons, and elite soldiers rode alongside ambassadors, nobles, merchants, and common travelers.

All of them were heading toward the same destination.

The Arena of the Five Kingdoms.

Evo leaned toward Bren and whispered, "I have never seen so many lords. I have also never seen horses that look as though they have bathed more recently than we have."

Tamsin lifted the edge of her cloak and sniffed it thoughtfully. "Everything has bathed more recently than we have."

The Queen overheard the remark and laughed quietly.

They caught their first glimpse of the arena at twilight.

Kade's breath caught in his throat.

Lira's eyes widened in silent awe.

Even Waylen's mouth fell open.

The arena stood within a vast valley that had been carved long ago by ancient magic. Its towering walls rose like jagged mountain ridges formed from stone and shimmering steel. Five colossal arches marked the entrances, each carved with the sigil of a kingdom.

Karthen's obsidian wolf.

Ylaria's silver serpent.

Veskain's storm eagle.

Oranth's blazing sun.

Thalen's twin moons.

The stands rose high above the valley floor, forming a colossal fortress capable of holding tens of thousands. Crystal lanterns hung from the arches and pillars, each glowing with blue fire that never dimmed.

Sound rolled toward them like waves crashing against a distant shore.

Crowds roared with excitement. Drums thundered in steady rhythm. Trumpets blared above the noise. Fires crackled in celebration across the valley.

Children raised carved wooden crowns high above their heads. Merchants shouted loudly about charms that promised victory in the arena. Priests lit sacred braziers that burned with ritual flame.

Kade suddenly felt very small beneath it all.

The immense scale of the arena pressed against him. Its long history, the weight of expectation, and the knowledge that the eyes of five kingdoms were turning toward him settled heavily on his shoulders.

His mother studied his expression carefully.

"It is overwhelming," she said gently. "It was the same for your father."

Kade glanced toward the King.

The King nodded once in agreement.

"I nearly fainted the first time I saw it," he admitted.

Waylen stared at him in disbelief. "You nearly fainted? Truly?"

"Of course," the Queen replied dryly. "He fainted directly into my lap."

Evo snorted loudly. "If Kade faints from nerves tomorrow, I will drag him straight into Lira's lap."

Lira drove her elbow into Evo's side with such force that he nearly toppled from his horse.

Nearby, the Priestess floated beside the crown that was carried between her moonstone guardians. Her voice drifted through the evening air, calm and steady.

"Welcome, heirs. Tomorrow the arena awaits."

The drums thundered again as thousands of voices rose together. The sound carried anticipation, hope, and a fierce hunger for spectacle.

Kade stared at the towering gates of the arena. His heart trembled somewhere between fear and destiny.

Beside him, Lira reached across and gently squeezed his hand.

Kade squeezed back.

CHAPTER THIRTY-SEVEN
The Night Before the Challenge

The Arena of the Five Kingdoms loomed behind them like a mountain of stone and steel, bathed in the last rays of the setting sun. Fires flickered in every archway, casting long shadows across the cobbled streets that led to the royal guest housing. The city hummed with restless excitement as soldiers and nobles hurried through the streets, preparing for the event that would decide the fate of five kingdoms.

Kade's horse nickered nervously as they approached the guest house. He felt the absence of the crown like a tangible weight pressing against his chest. It was not yet his and not yet within reach. The knowledge that tomorrow could end everything or finally begin it twisted his stomach into knots.

Beside him, Lira held his hand. Her fingers were cold but steady. She had stayed close all day, and her quiet presence grounded him even while his thoughts wrestled with doubt.

"You okay?" she asked softly. Her eyes searched his face for the slightest sign of unease.

He swallowed before answering. "I should be more afraid than I am. I keep thinking about what happens if I fail."

She squeezed his hand firmly. "You will not fail. You cannot. You are not alone. Not tomorrow and not ever."

"I know that," he said quietly. "But I still feel like I don't belong here. Sometimes it feels like I am playing a role that was meant for someone else."

"You belong," Lira said with certainty. "You were born for this. If the crown chose you, then it knows exactly what it's doing."

Kade's chest tightened. "And if I lose?"

"Then we will face that when the time comes," she replied calmly. "But we're not thinking about that right now."

They dismounted outside the royal guest house and handed their horses to waiting attendants. When they stepped inside, Kade's parents were already waiting near a hearth that burned brightly against the chill of the evening.

His mother stood with quiet grace, her gown shimmering softly in the firelight like the color of midnight clouds. Her eyes were bright with emotion. His father stood beside her. The king's armor rested on a stand nearby, and for once he appeared relaxed in a way that only happened when no court watched him.

"Kadeon," his father said, his voice carrying a depth of emotion that he struggled to contain. "I still cannot believe you are truly here."

Kade drew a slow, unsteady breath. "I never thought I would see you again."

"You were lost, but never forgotten," his mother said gently.

She stepped forward and wrapped him in a fierce embrace, holding him as though she could make up for twenty years of absence in a single moment.

"We prayed every day for this moment," she whispered.

Kade felt the warmth of her arms and the steady beat of her heart against his chest. Grief and relief tangled together inside him until he shivered.

"You have your mother's spirit," the king said as he stepped closer, "and you carry mine as well." His voice softened. "The blood of Karthen runs in you, Kadeon. Never doubt that."

Kade lowered his gaze. "I grew up believing I was no one. I thought my life had no meaning."

"Your life has always had meaning, even when you did not know it," his mother said. She brushed a hand gently through his hair. "Every choice you made and every hardship you survived brought you to this moment."

"And you did not arrive alone," the king added. "You brought allies with you. Friends who are... loyal beyond reason."

As if summoned by his words, Bren, Evo, and Tamsin burst into the room with their usual lack of restraint. Their entrance created more noise than the entire guest house had contained moments before.

Bren spread his arms dramatically. "Kadeon's personal entourage of chaos reporting for duty!"

Evo grabbed a nearby chair and lifted it like a royal scepter. "We promise to protect him," he declared solemnly. "Occasionally even from himself."

Tamsin spun once in the middle of the room before stopping and pointing toward Waylen, who stood stiffly near a pillar. "And we will also ensure that the prince over there," she said sweetly, "does not become too impressed with himself."

Waylen folded his arms and narrowed his eyes. "You will regret speaking in such irreverent tones."

Bren leaned casually against a tapestry. "Regret is for people with poor judgment, darling."

Tamsin sighed dramatically. "Honestly, these people are exhausting."

Even Kade could not suppress a laugh. His shoulders relaxed for the first time in hours.

Later that evening, when the noise of the gathering had finally quieted, Lira walked alone through the corridors of the guest wing. Torchlight flickered against the stone walls, casting long shadows that followed her every step.

Her thoughts churned relentlessly. She thought of the shard, of her role. Most of all, she thought of what might happen if Kade fell tomorrow.

She pressed a hand to her heart.

"I can't think like that," she whispered to herself. "I have to be strong."

In the main hall, Kade sat before the hearth, staring into the fire. Bren and Evo argued loudly nearby over who deserved the first bed.

Waylen appeared in the doorway, moving silently into the room. His tall frame was outlined in shadow, and his expression remained cold.

"You should rest, Karthen," Waylen said smoothly. "Tomorrow you will need more than loyal friends to survive."

"I don't sleep well when someone is trying to threaten me," Kade replied calmly without lifting his eyes from the fire.

Waylen stepped closer and lowered his voice. "You should feel fear. Tomorrow you will face a man who has trained his entire life to claim the crown. I do not falter."

Kade finally lifted his gaze. "I am not afraid of you," he said quietly. "I am afraid of failing the people who believe in me. That is a fear worth respecting."

Waylen blinked, surprised. The calm certainty in Kade's voice seemed to catch him off guard. For a long moment, he said nothing.

Bren suddenly leaned out from behind a chair.

"Careful, Waylen," he said with exaggerated concern. "don't choke on your own ego."

Evo snorted. "We should probably summon a healer in case his ego collapses."

Tamsin clapped her hands once. "Or at least a fan for dramatic fainting... Or hair flips. Whatever helps."

Waylen's face darkened with embarrassment. Without another word, he turned sharply and strode from the hall.

Kade allowed himself the smallest smile before the seriousness of tomorrow settled over him once more.

Later that night, he lay in the bed prepared for him in the Karthen royal wing. Lira rested beside him. His parents' chambers were only a short distance away, while Bren, Evo, and Tamsin continued to make far too much noise in the next room.

Through the open balcony doors, he could see the crown suspended within its protective field in the courtyard below. It pulsed faintly with light, almost like a heartbeat counting down the final hours before destiny demanded its due.

Kade closed his eyes.

Tomorrow the world would judge him. Tomorrow he would either rise or fall.

Lira's hand rested in his, steady and warm in the darkness. For the first time since leaving the Peaks, he felt ready.

The distant laughter of his friends outside the chamber reminded him of one simple truth.

Even kings need allies who refuse to be serious all the time.

CHAPTER THIRTY-EIGHT
The Challenge Begins

The morning sun cast a harsh glare across the Arena of the Five Kingdoms, turning the stone seats into a blaze of gold and silver. From the highest terraces, banners of all five realms snapped sharply in the wind, each bearing its sigil: serpents, twin moons, wolves, a blazing sun, and eagles. The crowd below, nobles, soldiers, merchants, and common folk alike, cheered with a deafening roar that rolled like thunder beneath the open sky.

At the far end of the arena, the gates creaked open.

Dust swirled across the sand as a column of royal guards marched forward. They carried shields and torches that glimmered in the sunlight. Behind them drifted the Priestess of the Peaks, her movement so smooth it seemed as though the air itself carried her. Six guardians clad in moonstone armor flanked her. Between them, held aloft by an unseen force, floated the Crown of Echoes.

The crown pulsed with a quiet, steady heartbeat.

That faint rhythm sent a ripple of anticipation through the thousands gathered in the stands.

Kade stood at the center of the arena floor, his Karthen cloak secured across his shoulders and his sword ready in hand. The leather of his boots creaked as he adjusted his stance and surveyed the vast arena around him. The air felt electric, thick with tension.

From the opposite gate, Prince Waylen stepped into the sunlight.

His armor gleamed like polished silver, reflecting the brightness of the day. Sunlight glinted sharply along the edge of his blade. His face remained composed and controlled, but his eyes burned with fierce determination and a trace of fear he would never allow anyone to see.

The crowd erupted once more.

"Karthen! Ylaria! Karthen! Ylaria!"

Their voices collided in a roaring tide that shook the banners overhead and echoed across the distant hills.

Kade allowed his gaze to flick briefly toward the floating crown before returning to his opponent. In the crowd, he spotted familiar faces. His mother sat rigid in her seat, one hand pressed tightly against her heart. His father stood beside her with unwavering posture, eyes locked firmly on his son.

Lira sat beside them. Her steady gaze met Kade's for a moment, grounding him.

The Priestess raised her staff.

Ancient magic amplified her voice so that it rang across every corner of the arena like the strike of a bell.

"The Challenge of the Five Kingdoms begins," she proclaimed. "Heirs of blood and destiny will duel. The victor shall wear the crown. The vanquished shall yield or die."

Her guardians shifted slightly, forming a living barrier around the crown. The relic glowed faintly, as if it sensed the gravity of the moment.

Waylen stepped forward.

"Are you ready, Karthen?" he called across the arena.

Kade met his gaze without hesitation. "I was born ready."

Steel rang through the air as their swords collided.

Kade moved first. He feinted to the right before striking low. Waylen parried smoothly, his polished blade clashing against Kade's with a sharp metallic crack. Sparks leapt briefly between them as the two men circled, measuring each other carefully and searching for weakness.

Waylen struck again, delivering a precise upward slash aimed toward Kade's shoulder.

Kade twisted aside and deflected the strike with the flat of his blade. He answered immediately with a swift jab toward Waylen's midsection. The prince stepped back with effortless grace, a brief grin flashing across his face as though he enjoyed the duel.

"You have skill," Waylen said while circling slowly. "Street fighting may have kept you alive, but technique is what wins crowns."

Kade did not respond with words.

Instead, he let the rhythm of the duel answer.

Every movement he made was deliberate. Each swing, parry, and sidestep carried the instinct born from years spent surviving ruthless streets. He fought with agility and improvisation, anticipating danger before it fully formed. It was a style that no royal instructor could have taught.

The crowd leaned forward as Kade ducked beneath a wide overhead strike and rolled across the sand. He rose in one fluid motion and slashed toward Waylen's leg.

The prince blocked just in time.

The impact rang loudly across the arena and sent vibrations through the ground beneath their feet.

Kade stepped back and steadied his breathing.

"You fight well, Waylen," he said quietly.

"Flattery will not save you," Waylen replied. "This is the arena. Only strength, skill, and courage matter here."

Kade shifted his stance slightly while watching the prince's movements with sharp focus. He noticed patterns in Waylen's attacks. The prince relied heavily on precision and rigid patterns. Those habits made him formidable, but they also made him predictable.

Kade could use that.

A subtle drop of his shoulder created the illusion of weakness.

Waylen lunged instantly.

The prince delivered a powerful sweeping strike that could have ended the duel in a single moment.

Kade stepped aside at the last possible instant. Waylen's blade cut through empty air before striking the sand with a spray of scattered grains.

The crowd erupted in a wave of cheers.

Some voices shouted for the heir chosen by destiny. Others rallied behind the prince raised within palace walls.

From their seats near the royal box, Bren shouted loudly. "Nice dodge! Street wisdom beats shiny armor every time!"

Evo leaned forward and called out. "Waylen! Careful with that ego. It is slowing you down!"

Tamsin added with a grin. "Karthen's boy fights better than any prince in those fancy schools!"

The prince stiffened, a faint flush coloring his cheeks, yet his eyes never wavered from Kade.

The duel intensified. Steel rang sharply as swords clashed again and again. Sparks flared with every strike, flashing like fire in the sunlight. Waylen's attacks were precise and lethal, each one honed through years of training, yet Kade moved with fluid unpredictability, slipping through the prince's rhythm as if he were dancing to a music only he could hear.

A sudden twist of Kade's wrist sent Waylen's sword flying from his grasp. It spun across the arena floor, skidding over sand and scattering a small spray of grains. The crowd gasped, a unified sound that rippled through the terraces.

Waylen froze, chest rising and falling as he struggled to catch his breath. Kade held his ground, taking no step forward. He extended a single hand toward the fallen sword.

"Yield," Kade said calmly, his voice carrying over the roar of the crowd, "or take it back."

Silence fell across the arena, thick and heavy. Waylen's jaw tightened, his gaze locking with Kade's in a long, measured stare. Then, a short, bitter laugh escaped him. With a sudden, fluid motion, he lunged for his sword.

The duel continued, each movement sharp, deliberate, and unrelenting. Minutes passed as the two heirs tested every skill, every instinct. Neither gave quarter, yet neither claimed victory. Finally, the signal horn blared across the arena, announcing the end of the first round.

The crowd erupted into a frenzy, their cheers and applause echoing from the terraces to the distant hills. Every shout praised the skill, the daring, and the courage of both heirs.

After a short break Kade and Waylen faced each other once more, circling slowly, each movement measured. They watched and breathed and searched for the slightest sign of weakness in the other. The sun dipped toward the horizon, casting long shadows across the sand. Above them, the banners snapped in the wind, and the Crown of Echoes hovered silently, pulsing with quiet, expectant energy. The final horn blew loud and long, signaling the end of the round.

In the stands, Kade's parents exchanged a glance that carried both pride and fear. Beside them, Lira had held her breath, her eyes locked on every swing, every block, and every agile pivot.

Tomorrow would bring another round. Another test. Another step toward the crown.

But for now, the arena had witnessed a single undeniable truth: Kadeon Vereth Karthen was no ordinary heir.

And the true battle had only just begun.

CHAPTER THIRTY-NINE
The Second Round

The sun rose over the Arena of the Five Kingdoms and painted the vast stone seats in streaks of fire and gold. Nobles, soldiers, and commoners from all five realms filled the stands. They leaned forward eagerly, drawn by the promise of the second day of the duel. Rumors of the brilliance of the first round had spread through every corner of the city, and the air hummed with anticipation.

The crown hovered above the center of the arena, suspended by the Priestess's guardians. It pulsed with a deep, resonant thrum that seemed to echo the collective heartbeat of the crowd.

Kade stepped onto the sand once more. His leather boots crunched softly against the pale arena floor. With his sword in hand, he lifted his gaze and scanned the stands. His parents sat among the spectators, their faces tense yet proud. Lira stood beside him for a brief moment, and her hand brushed his arm in a quiet gesture that reminded him he was not alone. Bren, Evo, and Tamsin leaned forward from their seats. They whispered warnings, jokes, and reckless bets that were loud enough for several rows of spectators to hear.

Across the arena, Waylen entered through the opposite gate. His armor gleamed in the morning light, and his expression was tight with focus. Beneath that focus, Kade sensed the prince's barely restrained frustration.

Lira moved toward the stands and took her seat beside Kade's parents just as the Priestess's voice rang across the arena.

"The second round begins," she declared. "Both combatants may select a secondary weapon from the stands. They will fight until one yields or falls."

Attendants pushed forward racks of weapons that gleamed in the sunlight. Axes, spears, short swords, and maces rested neatly upon the stands, each one polished and ready for battle.

Waylen's eyes moved toward a heavy spear resting against the rack. At the same moment, Kade's hand drifted toward a set of throwing knives strapped to the side of the display. A small smirk touched his lips as he tested their balance.

Waylen strode forward and lifted the spear with both hands. He gave it a quick and practiced flick as he tested its weight and flexibility. Kade selected the knives instead. They were light, perfectly balanced, and deadly in skilled hands.

The arena fell silent as the two combatants faced one another again.

Waylen attacked first. He lunged forward, and the spear swept through the air in a broad and dangerous arc. Kade twisted aside and rolled with the motion, allowing the prince's momentum to carry him forward. As he rose to his feet, Kade drew one of his knives and sent it spinning toward Waylen.

Waylen reacted instantly. He knocked the blade aside with the shaft of the spear. The sharp clash of steel rang through the arena like a thunderclap.

"You think quickly," Waylen said as he circled him. "But speed cannot outmatch reach."

Kade lowered himself into a relaxed stance and allowed a faint grin to appear. "Reach means nothing without thought."

He darted forward and feinted a strike. Then he rolled away again before Waylen could counter, forcing the prince to overextend and stumble half a step. With each movement, Kade's street bred cunning became more apparent. He used every advantage the arena offered. The shifting sand beneath their feet slowed heavier steps. The stone platforms along the edges offered brief moments of cover and elevation. Even the hanging banners cast shifting shadows across the ground that he used to mask his movements.

Waylen thrust, swung, and lunged with relentless precision. Each attack carried the power and discipline of a trained royal warrior. Yet every strike met careful evasion or a subtle trap created by Kade's positioning. Whenever Waylen pushed too far forward, Kade forced him back again and gradually turned the prince from hunter into defender.

From the stands, Bren cupped his hands around his mouth and shouted, "He is making you dance, Waylen. Try not to step on your own ego."

Evo leaned over the railing and added, "Remember your training, Prince. Does it include dodging unpredictability?"

Tamsin rose halfway from her seat and announced with theatrical flair, "Your armor may shine, but you rely on that shine to blind your opponent."

Laughter rippled through the crowd. The spectators roared with delight as the tension of the duel mingled with the thrill of the spectacle. Waylen's jaw tightened, and his grip on the spear hardened. The laughter of the crowd was something he could not ignore, and it gnawed at his composure in ways that Kade's blades could not.

Time blurred as the duel continued. Sand scattered beneath their feet as weapons clashed again and again, and the sun climbed steadily across the sky. Neither combatant yielded, and neither one fell.

At last, Kade saw his chance.

Waylen, exhausted and driven by mounting frustration, lunged forward with the spear one final time. Kade sidestepped the attack at the last instant. With a swift motion of his knives, he struck the spear aside and forced Waylen off balance.

Before the prince could recover, Kade closed the distance between them. He drove Waylen backward and forced him onto the sand. In the next heartbeat, Kade stood over him with both knives poised at Waylen's throat.

Waylen's eyes flicked toward the crown and then returned to Kade. The weight of realization settled across his face. He had lost the advantage.

The crowd held its collective breath.

With a reluctant exhale, Waylen slowly raised a hand in surrender. "I yield," he said, his voice strained but steady.

The arena erupted in cheers. Banners snapped violently in the wind as the sound rolled through the terraces. Kade's parents rose to their feet and applauded, pride shining plainly in their faces. Lira released a breath as relief softened her expression, though a trace of worry still lingered in her eyes as she watched the fallen prince.

Waylen's gaze burned with unspent fury.

As Kade turned to acknowledge the crowd and the officials of the arena, Waylen suddenly lunged. In one swift motion, he seized the spear he had just relinquished and hurled it with deadly precision.

"Look out!" Bren shouted, his eyes wide.

In the same instant, Bren hurled his axe. The weapon spun through the air with perfect aim and struck the spear in mid flight. The impact split the shaft apart in a burst of splintered wood and sparks, sending the broken fragments scattering harmlessly across the sand.

The crowd gasped. Lira's hand flew to her mouth.

Kade spun around with his sword raised, his heart pounding in his chest. Then he saw Bren standing at the edge of the arena with a sheepish grin.

"Never let your friends sit idle," Bren said with a shrug. "Someone has to keep the dramatic moments dramatic."

The Priestess raised her staff. A protective aura shimmered into existence around Kade as the crown pulsed with brighter light.

Waylen sank slowly to his knees, his chest rising and falling with heavy breaths. He was defeated, though still alive.

Kade stood tall at the center of the arena. He lowered his sword, sheathed his knives, and steadied his gaze.

The Arena of the Five Kingdoms erupted once more in thunderous cheers. Applause echoed across the terraces and carried down into the valleys beyond.

The Challenge was over.

Kade had proven himself worthy. The crown could finally recognize its rightful heir.

Lira stepped forward and grasped his arm. "You did it," she whispered.

Kade smiled, though exhaustion lined his face. "We did it," he replied. He glanced toward the stands where Bren, Evo, and Tamsin were celebrating with wild enthusiasm.

The Priestess's voice rang out above the noise.

"The crown shall be held by its rightful king. The laws of the Challenge have been fulfilled. The Five Kingdoms now await their sovereign."

In that moment, standing amid the roaring crowd, Kadeon Vereth Karthen understood something he had only begun to suspect before.

Destiny had not simply chosen him.

It had tested him, shaped him, and at last allowed him to rise.

CHAPTER FORTY
The Coronation

The Arena of the Five Kingdoms had been transformed overnight. Red, gold, and silver banners hung from the balconies and fluttered in the brisk morning air. The crowd stretched as far as the eye could see. Nobles, soldiers, and citizens from all five realms filled the stands, their attention fixed on the center of the arena, where a raised dais had been prepared for the coronation.

Above the dais floated the Crown of Echoes. The Priestess stood beside it with her unearthly guardians. The crown glowed like a captured sun, its rings of gold, silver, and midnight blue turning slowly in the air. Light shimmered across the spinning bands like fire reflected upon water.

Kade, clad in the ceremonial attire of Karthen royalty, stood at the base of the dais. Lira, Bren, Evo, and Tamsin stood beside him, forming a quiet circle of loyalty. Behind them stood the King and Queen of Karthen. Pride and relief shone openly on their faces as they watched their son.

Prince Waylen stood several steps away, still resplendent in his Ylarian armor. Though he had been defeated in the Challenge, he had been granted the courtesy of witnessing the coronation.

The Priestess stepped forward. When she spoke, her calm and resonant voice carried across the enormous arena.

"Kadeon Vereth Karthen," she intoned, "you have endured the trials of the Crown. You have faced the Challenge and proven your strength before the Five Kingdoms. You have shown courage, sacrifice, and honor. Kneel now and receive what destiny has placed before you."

Kade lowered himself onto one knee. For a brief moment, his gaze moved across the sea of faces. He saw his parents first. Then his eyes found Lira.

The crown descended slowly, as though measuring the weight of the moment. When it reached Kade, the spinning rings brightened. The gold, silver, and midnight blue bands aligned and settled upon his head. The light intensified for a heartbeat, as though the crown itself recognized its bearer.

A surge of radiant energy spread outward from the crown. The arena seemed to draw a breath as the light surrounded Kade like a mantle of living fire. The ancient relic had made its choice.

The crowd erupted. Cheers thundered through the arena with such force that the mountains beyond the city seemed to echo the sound.

The Priestess then turned her gaze toward Lira. She lifted her hands, and the shard embedded near Lira's heart pulsed faintly beneath her skin.

"And you," the Priestess said, her voice softer yet still carrying across the arena, "you carried the Shard of Choosing. Through courage, loyalty, and sacrifice, you safeguarded the power that guided the crown to its rightful king. The Crown of Echoes acknowledges your role in its destiny."

The shard glowed once more in response to the Priestess's words.

"You are the guardian of its will," the Priestess continued, "and the protector of the king whose fate you helped shape."

Lira stepped forward and bowed her head. A ripple of murmurs spread through the crowd. Some voices carried awe, while others carried unease as they witnessed the ancient magic unfolding before them.

Kade rose to his full height. The crown gleamed upon his head as he turned to face her.

"Lira," he said.

His voice remained steady, yet the emotion beneath it carried across the arena, which had suddenly fallen silent.

"You have been my anchor when the world turned against me. You have been my guide when I could not see the path ahead. You have carried the shard that bound our destinies together."

He reached out and gently took her hand.

"Before the Five Kingdoms, before the crown that has chosen me, and before every witness gathered here today, I ask you this. Will you stand beside me and become my queen?"

A deep silence settled across the arena.

Lira's heart pounded in her chest. Tears shimmered in her eyes, but her gaze never left Kade's.

Slowly and with quiet certainty, she stepped forward.

"I will," she whispered.

Then she lifted her voice so that every soul in the arena could hear her.

"I will."

The arena erupted into celebration. The roar of the crowd shook the very foundations of the stone coliseum. Fireworks ignited along the terraces in brilliant bursts of color, and the great banners snapped sharply in the rising wind.

Behind them, the King and Queen of Karthen wept openly with pride.

Prince Waylen watched the moment in silence. Bitterness still lingered in his expression, yet he inclined his head slightly in acknowledgment. The Challenge had been fought and decided. The crown had chosen its bearer.

The Priestess raised her staff once more, and the crowd slowly quieted.

Her gaze swept across the vast assembly.

"The Five Kingdoms bear witness," she declared. "The Crown of Echoes has recognized its true heir."

She turned toward Kade and Lira.

"Let this day mark the beginning of unity among the realms. Let justice guide the throne. Let the crown remember the sacrifices that restored it."

Her voice rose with solemn authority.

"All hail King Kadeon Vereth Karthen and Queen Lira of Karthen."

The roar that followed rolled across the arena like thunder.

The crown pulsed once more. Its rings spun faster for a brief moment before gradually slowing and settling into a steady and unwavering glow above Kade.

A respectful hush fell over the arena as Kade raised his hand, signaling the beginning of the formal proceedings.

"Citizens of Karthen. Citizens of the Five Kingdoms," he called. His voice carried across the arena, strong, confident, and resonant. "I stand before you today as your King. Together with Queen Lira, I swear that we will uphold the laws of the realm, defend the weak, and restore honor to the Crown. Let it be known that the Five Kingdoms shall flourish under our rule."

As he spoke, the crown brightened, its light pulsing in a quiet rhythm above him, as if responding to his words.

The arena erupted in celebration. Soldiers lifted their banners high into the air. Nobles bowed their heads in respect. Children leaned eagerly over the balconies, waving and cheering with unrestrained excitement. The sound of thousands of voices echoed off the stone walls, shaking the arena with joy.

Later, behind the royal dais, Kade met with his parents.

His father, King Vereth, stepped forward and placed a firm hand on his shoulder. Pride shone clearly in his eyes. "You have exceeded every hope, Kadeon," he said. "You are the prince we dreamed of, and far more than we ever imagined."

Queen Amara reached up and gently held Kade's face in her hands. Her voice was soft but certain. "You were never truly lost, my son. Destiny simply chose a different road to guide you home."

Kade nodded slowly. He glanced at Lira, who stood beside him, calm and radiant beneath the fading glow of the crown. "And I will never have to walk that road alone again," he said.

Nearby, Bren, Evo, and Tamsin were causing a minor disturbance among the gathered guests. The three of them loudly debated which of their jokes during the journey had been the most brilliant. Their argument drew a mixture of laughter and weary sighs from the royal attendants who were trying to maintain order.

Prince Waylen remained apart from the celebration. He stood near the edge of the chamber, watching quietly. He still had to answer for the former queens death. The bitterness that had once marked his expression had softened, replaced by something closer to reluctant respect.

Kade approached him and extended his hand. "You fought well," he said.

Waylen hesitated for a moment before accepting the gesture. "And you," he replied quietly, "are King."

The coronation concluded with music, banners, and the formal recognition of the Five Kingdoms and their new rulers.

High above the arena, the Crown of Echoes continued to glow. Its light remained steady and unbroken, a symbol that the realm's destiny had been fulfilled and that a new future had only just begun.

EPILOGUE
The Royal Wedding and the New Court

The sun rose over Karthen, spilling gold across the capital's towers and the emerald forests beyond. Banners fluttered in the gentle morning breeze, and the streets were alive with celebration. Citizens from all Five Kingdoms had gathered not only to witness the union of their new king and queen but also to mark the beginning of an era they had long hoped to see.

Kade stood at the altar of the grand cathedral, the Crown of Echoes resting upon his head once more. This time, it was not a symbol of a Challenge won, but the mark of a reign that had truly begun.

Lira approached slowly, her gown woven with threads that caught the sunlight like liquid silver. The fabric shimmered with every step, drawing the eyes of every noble and commoner alike.

When their eyes met, the memory of trials, duels, and mountain winds seemed to vanish into the distance. For a brief moment, the world beyond the cathedral ceased to matter. There were only the two of them, their hearts aligned and their fates bound together.

"I, Kadeon Vereth Karthen," Kade intoned, his voice carrying across the gathered crowd, "take you, Lira, as my Queen. Together we will lead, protect, and honor these kingdoms with courage and wisdom."

"I, Lira," she replied, her voice steady and clear, "stand beside you as your Queen, your anchor, and your partner in all that lies ahead."

The cathedral erupted with cheers. Trumpets blared as confetti of silver and gold rained from the balconies above. Citizens of Karthen, Ylaria, and the other kingdoms lifted their voices in celebration, waving banners and shouting in joy. The union of their rulers promised unity, strength, and hope for the entire realm.

After the ceremony concluded, the royal court assembled for the announcement of the King and Queen's council. Kade stepped forward, a sly grin tugging at the corner of his mouth.

"Every king and queen needs a council," he said, his eyes glinting with amusement. "And every ruler deserves friends who can fight, think, and occasionally cause chaos with remarkable flair."

He gestured toward Bren, Evo, and Tamsin, who stood near the edge of the dais. They attempted to look dignified and composed, but the effort was clearly failing.

"You three," Kade continued, "will serve in my court. Bren, you will oversee the Royal Guard and ensure the security of the crown. Evo, you will serve as head of royal intelligence and tactical strategy, reporting directly to me. And Tamsin..." He turned to her with a knowing grin. "You will manage the training of the palace elite and serve as chief advisor on matters that require both wit and diplomacy."

The three exchanged astonished looks before their restraint completely collapsed. Cheers and triumphant whoops echoed through the cathedral.

"You're making us officials?" Bren asked, his voice filled with disbelief and awe.

"Yes," Lira said with a warm smile. "And you are already spectacular at it."

"Of course I am," Evo muttered, his eyes sparkling with pride.

Tamsin placed a hand over her heart and bowed theatrically. "At last, the recognition I deserve."

Kade raised his hand for silence, and the murmurs in the hall faded.

"With them at my side," he declared, his voice carrying through the chamber, "and with all of you gathered here today, the Five Kingdoms shall know a reign built on fairness, strength, and courage. Let this court stand as a reminder that loyalty and friendship are as vital to a kingdom as bloodlines and crowns."

The crowd erupted into cheers once more, louder than ever. The new King and Queen of Karthen stepped down from the dais together, their hands clasped, their hearts steady, and their destinies finally fulfilled.

Later, as the sun sank beneath the horizon, the royal wedding feast began in the grand hall. Candles flickered along the long tables, music rose in joyous harmony, and laughter echoed from every corner of the chamber.

Kade and Lira moved among the crowd, greeting nobles and citizens alike. Their smiles never faltered, and the strength of their unity was evident to all who watched.

Bren, Evo, and Tamsin, now formally welcomed into the royal court, stood close by. They watched the celebration with pride, sharing laughter and already plotting new ways to keep their king and queen entertained and occasionally on their toes.

High above the city, the moon rose and spilled silver light across the rooftops of Karthen. From the mountains to the valleys, across forests and winding rivers, the Five Kingdoms witnessed the dawn of a new era. It was an era forged in trials, sealed in love, and secured by the bonds of friendship that had carried a lost prince to his crown and a shard-bearer to her destiny.

* 9 7 9 8 9 5 0 0 8 2 2 5 2 *